Sigillagraphia

Illustrated History Of Magic Symbols

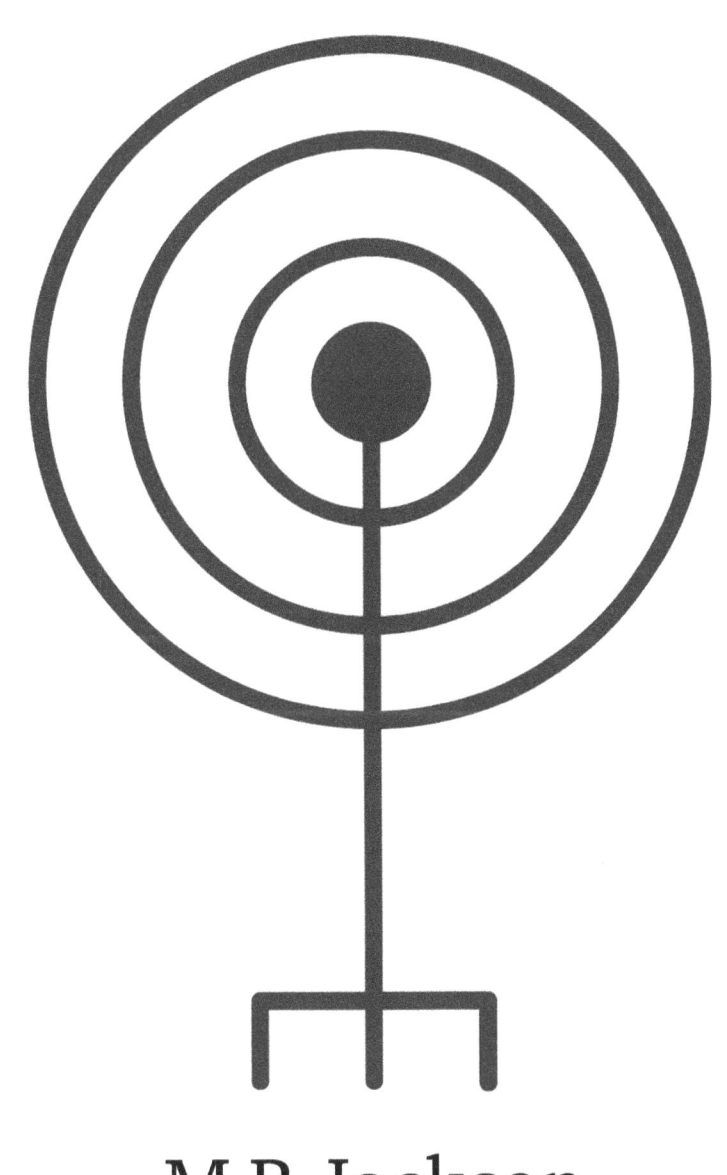

M B Jackson

GREEN MAGIC

Sigillagraphia © 2023 by Mark Jackson.
All rights reserved. No part of this book may be used or reproduced
in any form without written permission of the Author,
except in the case of quotations in articles and reviews.

GREEN MAGIC
Seed Factory
Aller
Langport
Somerset
TA10 0QN
England
www.greenmagicpublishing.com

COVER IMAGE: Atlantean Menorah

Print origination by Carrigboy, Wells, UK.
www.carrigboy.co.uk

ISBN 978 1 915580 04-7

GREEN MAGIC

Contents

Magic Symbolism 6

Prehistory 70,000–3000 BCE 12

Ancient World 3000–1500 BCE 18

Classic World 1500 BCE–600 CE 24

Medieval World 600–1450 32

Renaissance World 1450–1600 40

Modern World 1600–1945 58

Post Modern World 1945–2025 82

Sigil Craft 110

Further Reading 121

Magic Symbolism

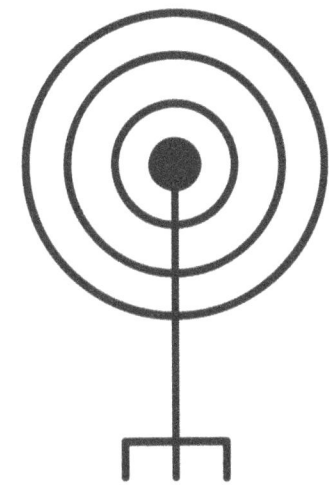

Magic Symbolism

The mystery language of magic is symbolism. It is a language we all recognize but few of us are fluent in. The majority of symbols that exist today were created long ago. They represent the movements of heaven and earth, the four seasons, and cosmic and earthly deities. Over time, they have acquired layers of increasingly complex meaning.

Symbols are the way our ancestors took all information as energy and put it into images. The oldest signs with meaning are the dot and the line, or egg and sperm. They are the parents from which all others have evolved.

These two parent signs, plus their five offspring, make a family of seven basic signs that form all other signs. The dot, line and circle are the most elementary of these. A dot can be expanded to form a circle, which can be bisected by a vertical or horizontal line to create two from one or to represent the horizon. A dot sign can have lines drawn through its center to represent the four, or eight, compass points that form an asterisk or star pattern.

The dot, or point, signifies unity, the origin, source or beginning. The circle is the dot expanded to infinity, symbolizing the Universe, eternity, unity, eternal motion, the abyss and nothing.

An arc is a bisected circle. The upper section is symbolic of the rising sun and the rainbow. The lower section forms the basis of all lunar symbols; it represents the feminine, passive, receptive principle, symbolic of the womb and chalice.

The line, drawn with a single stroke, can be straight, wavy or zigzag. The vertical line is the active, dynamic principle: the body erect. The horizontal line represents the passive, static principle: the body supine. The oblique line is halfway between the vertical and the horizontal. A wavy line and a zigzag are not the same. A wavy line is fluid and passive; the zigzag is sharp, jagged and abrupt.

There are a select few open signs that retain their original esoteric meaning across all human cultures from prehistory. The most revered of these is the 'sign of signs', better known as the Cross.

In its upright form it represents protection, honour, balance, structure, sacredness, unification, choice and the points of the compass. In its diagonal form it represents protection and the four seasons. Superimposed over one another they form the eight-rayed star – the archaic symbol for God, heaven and king. Both forms of cross can be extended to render the swastika.

The arrow is an expression of movement and direction, pointing the way, and is used to symbolize life and death. When two forked signs are combined, they create symbols that attract and repel each other.

The spiral is a single, curved, non-crossing open line that is radially symmetrical. Its primary function is to describe the origin of the Universe by following the path of the Sun, symbolizing expansion, contraction, creativity, the feminine, a journey.

Closed signs refer to geometric shapes (e.g. circle, square, triangle and star) to distinguish them from open signs such as the cross, arrow and spiral. Hermetic magic employs geometric shapes as functional magic and, paired with ritual magic, is used in the creation of pendants, amulets, talismans, mandalas, cosmograms and other schema.

The circle expands outwards to represent beginning, potential, motion, cosmos, eternity and protection. The triangle represents creation, manifestation and illumination. The square is passive, representing the male order and symbolizing the earth, land, field, ground, foundation, security and structure. The four points of the compass represent the four seasons.

Compound signs are always composed of two or more basic signs. By welding or binding together basic, open and closed signs, more complex symbols can be developed.

Complex signs such as cosmograms (like mandalas and yantras) are made up of a multitude of open and closed signs, which together produce an expression that is too complex and opaque to be considered a sign. Rather, it is a schema; an underlying organizational pattern or structure.

Schema is a Greek term meaning shape or

plan. It is used to describe a diagrammatic representation, or pattern, imposed on complex reality or experience to assist in explaining it, to mediate perception, or to guide response. It is a simplified abstract view of the complex reality whose proposed scope is the known and the knowable.

One such schema is an ancient cosmogram called the Flower of Life (the modern name for a symbol of Sacred Geometry), which is composed of evenly spaced overlapping circles, arranged so that they form a flower-like pattern. As more circles are added, the pattern emerges to depict the fundamental forms of time and space.

Also called the Language of Silence and the Language of Light, the figure is constructed from a combination of basic signs – female circle signs that have male straight lines imposed upon them to reveal the hidden structures of the universal consciousness.

The discipline known as Sacred Geometry revolves around the idea that all consciousness, including human, is solely based on Sacred Geometry. According to Thoth, all levels of consciousness in the Universe are integrated by a single image in Sacred Geometry. It is the key to time, space, dimension, consciousness, emotion and thought.

The symbol is found all over the world – in China, Tibet, Japan, Egypt, Israel, Turkey, Greece, Britain and Ireland. From the early Middle Ages 600 CE, it became a part of the Hermetic tradition of Western occultism.

As a symbol of Sacred Geometry, it contains ancient religious values. In this sense, it is a visual expression of the connections life weaves through all sentient beings, an Akashic record of the basic information of all living things.

It is the primal language of the Universe; pure shape and proportion. It is called a flower not just because it looks like a flower but because it represents the cycle of a fruit tree. The fruit tree makes a little flower, which metamorphosizes into a fruit. The fruit contains within it the seed, which falls to the ground and then grows into another tree. Thus, the symbol reflects the cycle composed of tree to flower to fruit to seed and back to tree.

This cycle can be defined within the Flower of Life by several other geometric figures, including the Seed of Life, which also contains the Tree of Life and the Egg of Life. The Fruit of Life contains Metatron's Cube, which contains all the Platonic Solids.

The Seed of Life is a construct of seven interconnected circles placed within a sixfold symmetry, which acts as the base component of the middle of the Flower of Life. In the Judeo-Christian tradition, the stages which construct the Seed of Life are said to represent the Seven Days of Creation. The first step in creating the Seed was the creation of a two-dimensional circle (in some religions, it is an octahedron). The next step was to spin the circle on its axis to form a three-dimensional sphere which contains the creative conscious.

In the Flower of Life and the Seed of Life can be found another pattern called the Tree of Life, or the Sephirotic Tree of Jewish cabala. As a cabalistic concept, the Sephirotic Tree is used to understand the nature of God and the manner in which He created the world out of himself, using the letters of the alphabet. Cabalists developed the concept into a full model of reality, using the tree to depict a map of creation. Within the flower pattern, the tree is surrounded by the Star Tetrahedron (or Star of David) and, whether it is coincidence or not, all the letters of the Hebrew alphabet can be formed on the hexagram.

The Egg of Life is formed from the seven circles of the Seed of Life that form the centre of the Flower of Life. It is the shape of a multicellular embryo in its first hours of creation.

The Fruit of Life is composed of thirteen circles forming a six-rayed star of five circles in all directions. This star shape is said to be a blueprint of the Universe, containing the basis for the design of every atom, molecular structure, lifeform and everything in existence. It is the foundation of Metatron's Cube, which generates the five Platonic Solids. The Platonic Solids correspond to the five elements: Hexahedron/Cube – earth; Tetrahedron/Pyramid – fire; Octahedron – air, Icosahedron – water; Dodecahedron – ether/spirit.

SIGILLAGRAPHIA

MAGIC SYMBOLISM

Flower of Life

Seed of Life

Egg of Life superimposed on the Seed of Life

Tree of Life with two extra sephiroth superimposed on the Flower of Life

Tree of Life superimposed on the Seed of Life

Tree of Life surrounded by the Star Tetrahedron in the Egg of Life

Fruit of Life

Metatron's Cube

Platonic Solids

Sacred Geometry - Flower of Life

SIGILLAGRAPHIA

Universal Magic Symbols

Prehistory, Ancient World and Classic World
70,000 BCE–600 CE

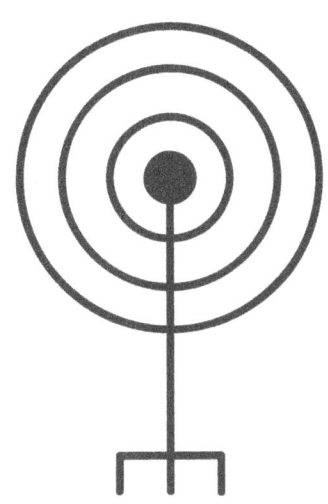

Prehistory 70,000–3000 BCE

The earliest date archaeologists have for the beginning of human mark-making is 70,000 BCE, with tally marks used to count the number of days for calendar making. These marks were usually simple dot and line notches in wood and bone. Called 'talking sticks', they are the first form of measuring device – the origin of the ruler.

The figurative art of prehistory includes the enigmatic scenes of wild animals from the caves of Spain and France, which were created between 40,000 and 30,000 BCE. Most famous for their scenes of wild animals, they may also feature the first depictions of the shaman or even the deity.

It is theorized that they involved rituals of sympathetic magic, designed to ensure a good hunt, or they were produced under the influence of hallucinogenic substances during shamanic rituals. Another recent theory suggests the caves are filled with light during the summer solstice and the paintings represent the zodiac created during the Age of Taurus.

In the earliest forms of prehistoric art, circa 40,000 BCE, the human figure is represented by the sculptured Venus figurines. Their purpose is debated, with opinion ranging from pornography to socially functional depictions of women created by women.

Often cited as the first depiction of a deity, the Sorcerer is one of the names given to an enigmatic cave painting found in France dating from around 13,000 BCE. A copy of this cave art was drawn by Henri Breuil, who asserted that the cave painting depicted a shaman or magician performing a hunting magic ritual. Some scholars dispute this, claiming the cave painting lacks the antlers shown in the drawing, thereby discounting the theory that the Sorcerer was evidence of a horned god that dated back to Paleolithic times.

The taking of hallucinogenic mushrooms to commune with the spirit world has been a part of shamanic ritual for millennia. Drawings of shaman, symbolized by their mushroom-shaped heads, have been found in cave art from the Neolithic period onwards.

Shamanism grew out of the Stone Age reindeer culture that was developed in Siberia by those hunting wild reindeer, or those who maintained domesticated deer. During the hunting magic ceremony, the hunter would put on a deer skin and antlers and imitate deer behavior. They prayed for success, using their bow and arrows as an accompaniment in these rituals – the bow and the antlers became symbols of their magic power.

The wearing of animal skins for ritual practices is called 'Skin Walking' by Native Americans. It is a concept in which the shaman takes on an animal form—such as a deer—by wearing its skin or hide, allowing a totemic ancestor to come to the people's world in the figure of a man whilst the shaman enters the ancestor's world in the guise of a deer.

These are the probable prototypes for an antlered deity that appeared during the Bronze Age and developed during the Iron Age as the Celtic God called Cernunnos.

In Neolithic symbolism circa 5000 BCE, Indalo was perceived to be a go-between between man and God – the rainbow providing a bridge between Heaven and Earth.

As opposed to the figurative art of prehistory, the concept of universal figures is even more apparent in geometric cave art. Such basic but meaningful abstract forms, based on geometric shapes, are the beginning of all written communication between gods and men, and men and men.

One of the most common geometric motifs found throughout the prehistoric world is the spiral. It dates from the painted and engraved walls of the Upper Paleolithic to the decorated megalithic standing stones of the Neolithic Era.

The spiral represents many ideas, such as the Sun, life, path of life, eternity, creation, reproduction cycle or even a portal to the spirit world. It featured heavily in the religious art of the Picts and Celts, and was expressed in many forms.

The swastika is one of the oldest examples

of a celestial sign. The oldest known version, dated from around 15,000 BCE, was carved into a mammoth tusk and employed as a symbol of fertility and regeneration.

Its unique form is derived from our ancestors' observation that the celestial North Pole star (or Polaris) never moved, and that the heavens revolved around it, marking the point in the heavens where God lived.

To accurately find Polaris, the top right hand star within the Little Dipper constellation was used to trace a line toward it. By marking the position of the Little Dipper through the seasons at the compass points, with Polaris at its center, a swastika was formed.

In Neolithic times, the symbol was common to all mankind as the Wheel of Life, representing the rotation of the heavens through the solar year divided by the four cardinal directions and the four seasons.

Our modern notion of the sign begins with its Indo-European roots as the swasti, "sw – good", and "asti – to exist", symbolizing the Wheel of Life, fertility, regeneration and good fortune.

After millennia of unchanged archaic tradition, the Nazi Party adopted it as their logo. Since then, it has been culturally cast as a symbol representing an ultimate of evil.

Variations of the solar aspect of swastika are the Sun Wheel and Sun Cross. These symbols were used to represent thunder, power and energy. In astrology, the Sun Cross is the symbol representing the planet and element of Earth.

Because it was the symbol of the Sun, kingship and the highest spiritual power, it was easy for early Christians to adopt this pagan symbol and incorporate it into the Latin Cross, as in the Celtic Cross, with its arms protruding beyond the circle.

After examining hundreds of Ice Age cave sites across Europe, paleoarchaeologist Genevieve von Petzinger discovered that our ancestors used 32 signs repeatedly. The oldest of which—a red disc the size of a saucer—is estimated to be at least 41,000 years old.

She compiled a database of geometric signs found at the 370 rock sites situated across the European continent. The use of these signs spanned 30,000 years of human habitation and sign-making.

She suggests that 32 of the many geometric signs accompanying such paintings are repeated and combined in such a way that they could be understood as messages, or even spells.

The symbols include the 'negative hand', one of the oldest types of imagery in the world, made by placing a hand on a wall and spitting paint over it to leave an outline.

These Ice Age signs were the ancestors of the ideogram and pictogram. Ideograms are signs that represent an idea like creation, life or eternity. Pictograms represent objects such as the Sun, water, trees, animals, buildings, tools and weapons; or actions, like run, carry, wave, welcome, halt, give, receive, think, etc.

The oldest existing ideograms and pictograms date to around 5500 BC. Called Vinča writing, or Old European Script, they were created by Neolithic people living around Vinča in Romania.

The signs are found on a number of artefacts called the Tărtăria Tablets, after Tărtăria in Transylvania where they were found. These European signs are similar in character to the earliest Middle Eastern pictographic script, but predate such writing systems by 2000 years.

The Vinča culture disappeared around 4000 BCE and it is possible that their pictograms were transported to the first civilizations of Sumer and Egypt in the form of astrolabes, star charts and zodiacs incised into clay, bark and metal.

Around 3000 BCE, the first examples of pictographic script began to appear in the first civilizations to enable the writing of kings' names, short messages in dedications to the gods and in incantations. These early pictographic scripts evolved into the cumbersome hieroglyphic systems of the ancient world.

Around 1050 BCE, the Phoenicians took elements from these ancient writing systems and the lunar calendar to create the first alphabet, from which all modern alphabets – including magic ones – are descended.

SIGILLAGRAPHIA

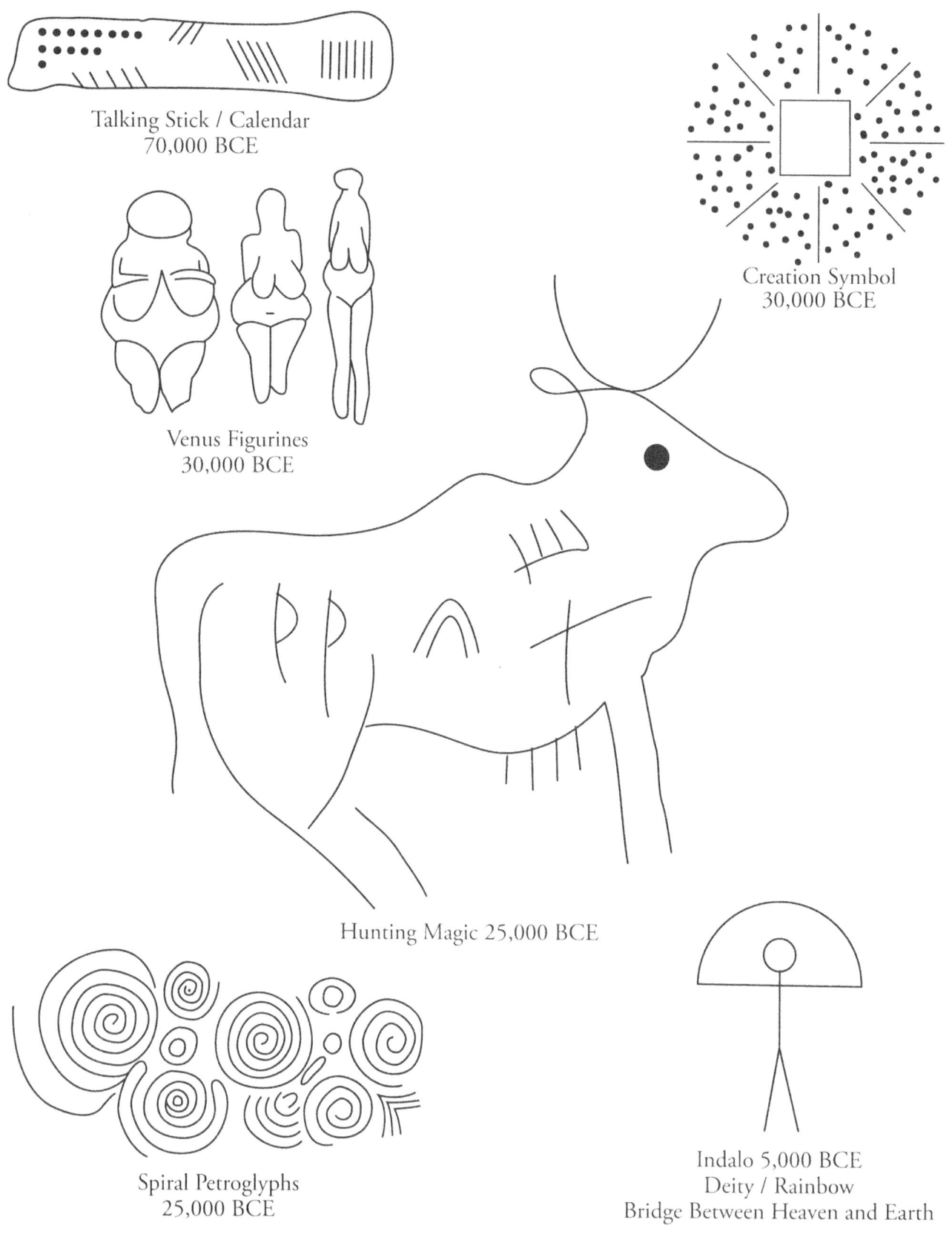

Talking Stick / Calendar
70,000 BCE

Creation Symbol
30,000 BCE

Venus Figurines
30,000 BCE

Hunting Magic 25,000 BCE

Spiral Petroglyphs
25,000 BCE

Indalo 5,000 BCE
Deity / Rainbow
Bridge Between Heaven and Earth

Stone Age Petroglyphs

PREHISTORY

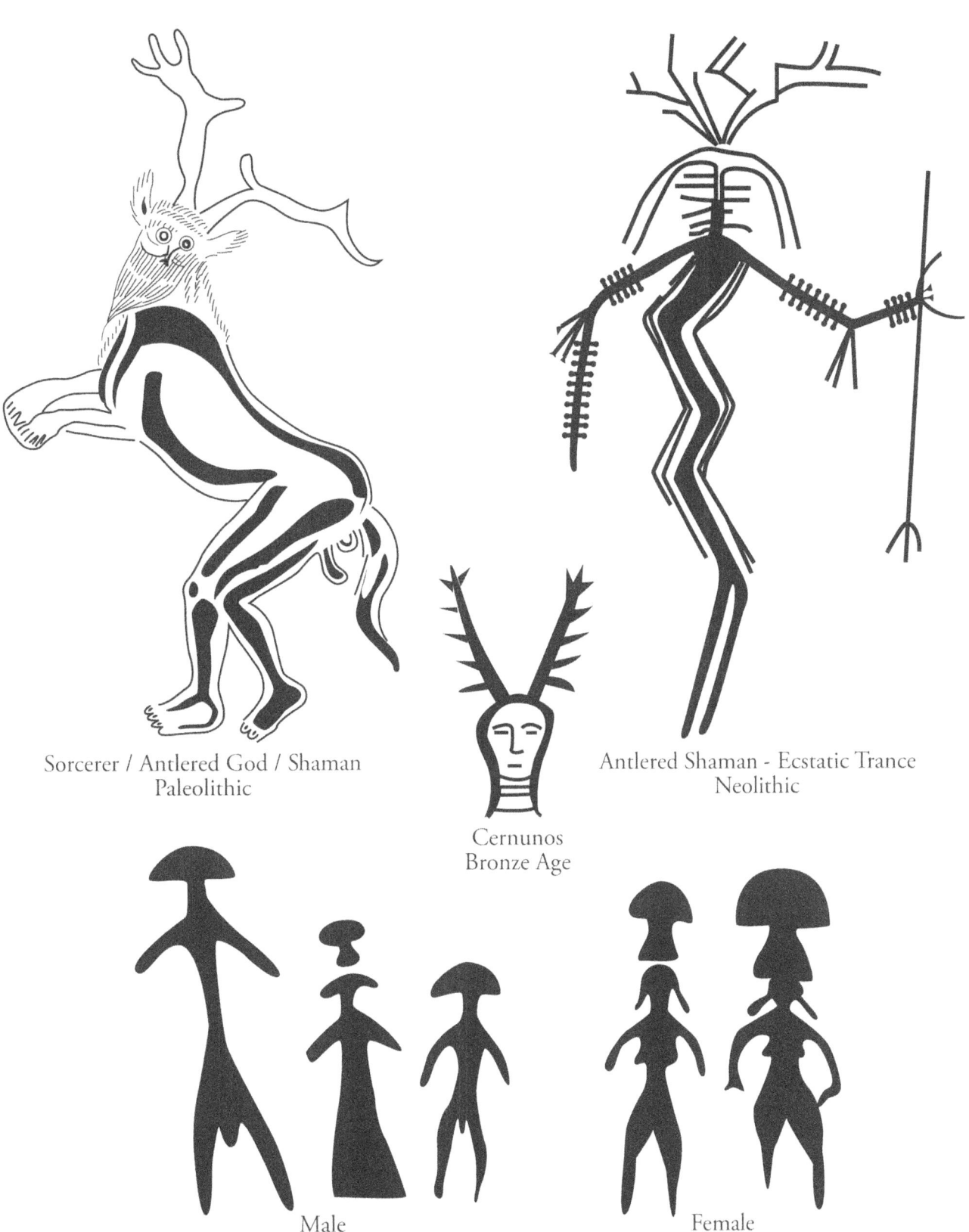

Sorcerer / Antlered God / Shaman
Paleolithic

Cernunos
Bronze Age

Antlered Shaman - Ecstatic Trance
Neolithic

Male

Female

Mushroom Shaman - Neolithic

Antlered Deity and the Shaman

SIGILLAGRAPHIA

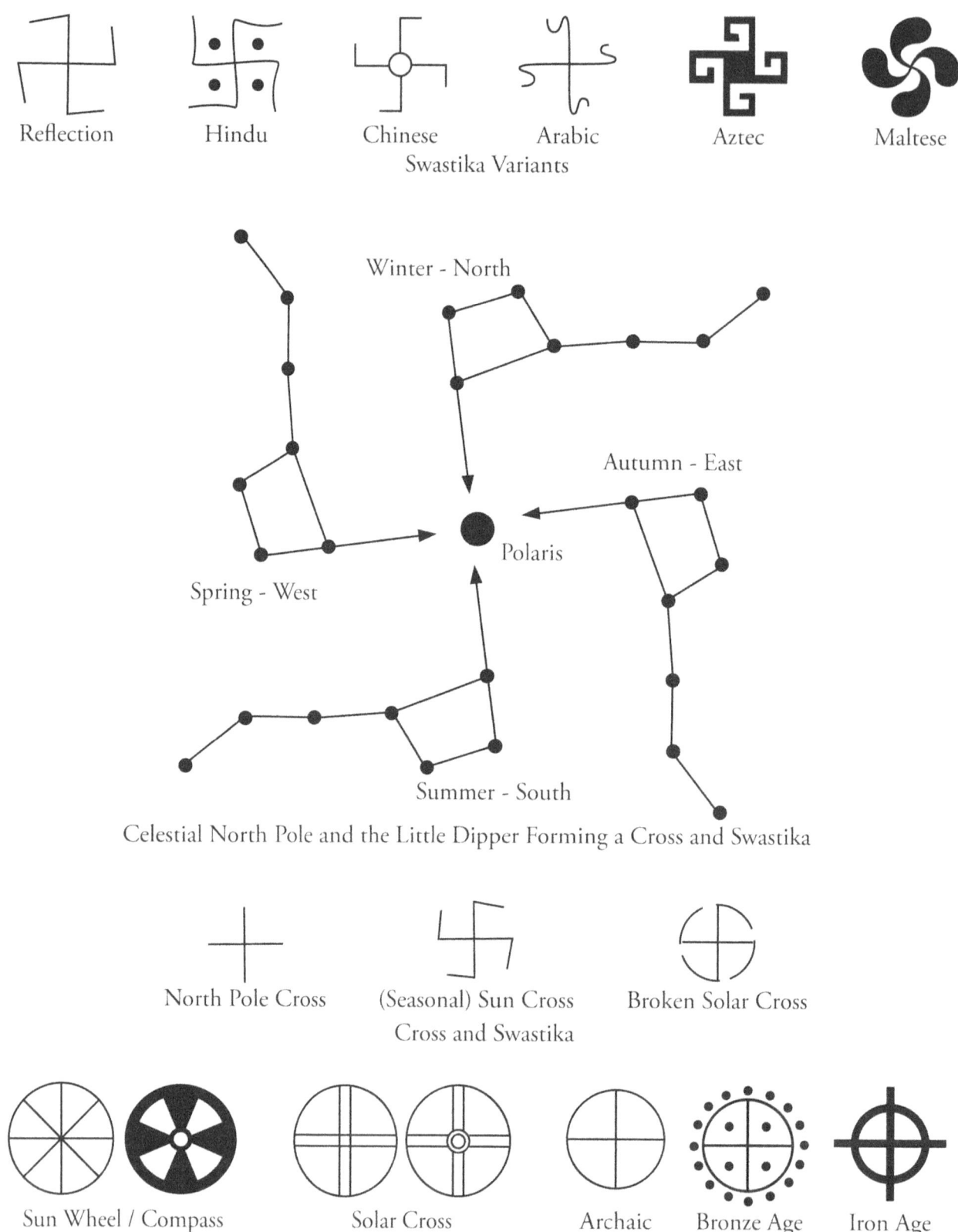

Swastika Variants: Reflection, Hindu, Chinese, Arabic, Aztec, Maltese

Celestial North Pole and the Little Dipper Forming a Cross and Swastika

Cross and Swastika: North Pole Cross, (Seasonal) Sun Cross, Broken Solar Cross

Sun Wheel and Solar Cross: Sun Wheel / Compass, Solar Cross, Archaic, Bronze Age, Iron Age

Swastika, Sun Wheel and Solar Cross

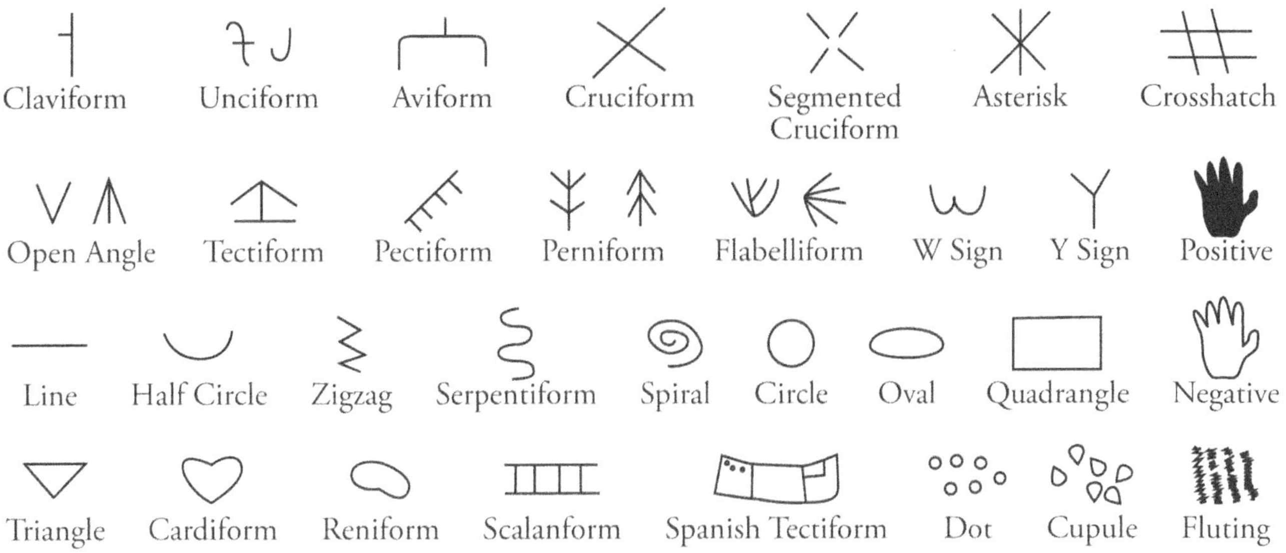

PREHISTORY

32 Meaningful Signs from Ice Age Europe

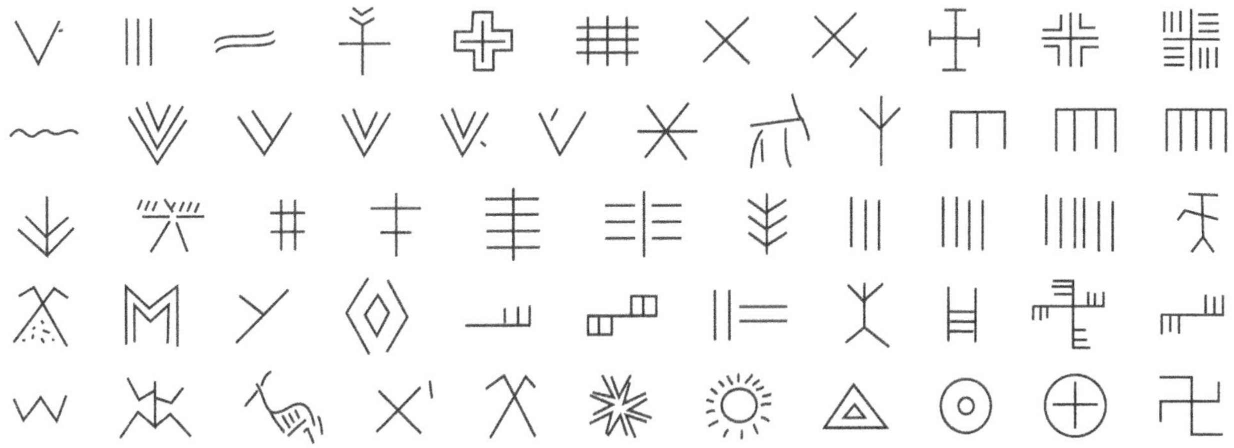

Claviform · Unciform · Aviform · Cruciform · Segmented Cruciform · Asterisk · Crosshatch

Open Angle · Tectiform · Pectiform · Perniform · Flabelliform · W Sign · Y Sign · Positive

Line · Half Circle · Zigzag · Serpentiform · Spiral · Circle · Oval · Quadrangle · Negative

Triangle · Cardiform · Reniform · Scalanform · Spanish Tectiform · Dot · Cupule · Fluting

Old European Ideograms and Pictigrams (Vinca) 5500 BCE

Neolithic Zodiacs and Star Maps 5,000 BCE

Common Elemental Letter Signs

Meaningful Signs from Prehistoric Europe

Ancient World 3000–1500 BCE

At the beginning of civilization it is likely that technological innovations, such as pottery and architecture, were canvasses for the reproduction of magic symbols from prehistory into the ancient world and beyond.

In a largely illiterate society, symbols serve the vital purpose of relaying the most important values of the culture to the people, generation after generation – and so it was in the ancient world.

Peasant farmers would have been unable to read the literature, poetry and hymns which told the stories of their gods, kings and history, but they could look at an obelisk or a relief on a temple wall and read them through the symbols used.

In a time when everything was magic, the world was full of mystery. People asked questions like, "Who are we? Where do we come from? Why are we here?" which led to the creation of organized religion.

Religion in the ancient world was fully integrated into people's lives. The gods were present at birth, throughout life and in the transition from earthly life to the eternal, and they continued to care for the soul in the afterlife. The spiritual world was ever-present in the physical world.

This understanding was symbolized through images in art, architecture, amulets, statuary and the objects used by the nobility and clergy in the performance of their duties.

Magic in the ancient world was predominantly aimed at maintenance and stability and involved a combination of ritual actions, symbolic imagery, performative recitation, written text and appropriate material ingredients.

Many practices of the ancient world that we today label 'magic' had exact intention behind them for influencing the course of events – to promote healing, offer protection, find love and compel the gods and spirits.

Babylon was just one of many empires in the Middle East that derived its culture from Sumer, the world's first civilization. This culture was influenced by that of the Chaldeans, or Star Gazers – a very ancient Semitic people who settled in Babylon. Abraham was a Chaldean high priest from the Babylonian city of Ur, whose ruling deity was the Moon God called Nanna/Sin, the Bull of Heaven.

By using symbols, people managed to identify the divine nature of the gods. Of these personal icons, the most often reproduced appear on four seals whose star symbolism was used to signify various members of the family of Enlil. Enlil was Commander in Chief of the Anunnaki Sky Gods on Earth, and was identified by the pentagram.

Enlil's first-born son, Nanna/Sin, was represented by the Crescent Moon. Nanna/Sin's first born son, Utu/Shamash, was the Sun God and his twin sister, Inanna/Ishtar, was Venus. They are the Gemini twins. The seals used to identify the gods appeared on cylinder seals, pottery, architecture and protective amulets.

Babylonian/Chaldean magic was the first system to attach godly, planetary, celestial and numerical correspondences to the letters of the alphabet – to divine fate and destiny using numerology and astrology.

It was also the first system to develop true names. In Babylonian mythology, chaos existed because nothing had a name. So they conceived the idea of ascribing a numerical value to each sign in their syllabary so that every name was capable of numerical expression. This is the beginning of cabala.

In Babylon, amulets made from different materials were worn around the neck as safeguards against disease, demons and misfortune. They were often engraved with images of divinities and always had talismanic formulae and incantations written on them. Magic conjurations included disrespectful incantations against evil spirits and the effects of sorcery, disease and misfortune.

Heka was the Egyptian God of Magic and Medicine. Using magic texts containing spells for treating diseases or injury, the ancient Egyptians used Heka or magic to empower hieroglyphs for amulets, talismans, magic figures and spells created by priests, magicians, healers, scorpion charmers, midwives, nurses and protection-makers.

Among the magic doctors were seers; people

who could see the future and could memorize spells for later use. Most Egyptians were illiterate and, in daily life, every class of Egyptian society wore amulets and talismans for protection. They also carried protective and healing spells that were written on papyrus, folded and worn against the body.

In ancient Egypt, the Wadjet or Eye of Horus was the most popular symbol. It was followed by the Scarab, the Ankh, the Djed, the Was, the Shen, the Ajet and others. These other symbols were frequently paired or associated with the three most often used – the Ankh, the Djed and the Was – and adorned the items Egyptians used in their daily lives.

The Wadjet first appeared as the symbol of the protective Goddess Wadjet and remained so, even though it was later more frequently associated with Ra, Horus and others.

As the Eye of Ra, it symbolized her presence over creation and is said to gather information for Ra. As the Eye of Horus, it is a stylized eye that possibly mimicked the facial markings of a falcon local to Egypt (Horus was symbolized by the falcon). The difference between the Eye of Horus and the Eye of Ra is that the Eye of Horus looks to the left, whereas the Eye of Ra looks to the right.

Khepher, or the Scarab Beetle, is one of the most frequently seen Egyptian symbols. The ancient Egyptians noticed that these 'dung beetles' had a practice of shaping balls of dung and rolling them to their nests to lay their eggs in them. They came to believe that the sun 'ball' was also rolled across the sky by the scarab-headed god Khepri, who was tasked with the job of helping the Sun to rise every morning and rolling it across the sky through the day.

The Scarab wasn't used exclusively to represent Khepri. It was a universal symbol representing the renewal of the day, life after death, immortality, resurrection, transformation, creation and protection. Scarab amulets were very popular and some featured winged scarabs.

The three most important symbols—the Ankh, Djed and Was scepter—often appeared in all manner of Egyptian artwork, from amulets to architecture. They were frequently combined in inscriptions and often appeared on sarcophagi, either together in a group or separately.

Ankh is Latin for 'cross with handle' and symbolizes the Key of Life. It is one of the most well-known symbols of ancient Egypt and is carried by the gods in their right hand. The general meaning of the symbol is Eternal Life, corresponding to the soul instead of the body.

The Djed column represents stability. It was often displayed in combination with the Was scepter and the Ankh, which created a combined meaning of strength, success and long life.

The Was scepter represents a ceremonial staff held by various gods, particularly Anubis and Set. It was a symbol of power and rulership, as is common with ceremonial scepters.

The Tjet – Tiet – Tyet/Knot of Isis, also known as the Buckle of Isis, Blood of Isis and Knot of Isis is a feminine symbol thought to resemble a piece of cloth that has been looped and then knotted. The symbol is found on funerary amulets, carved into the walls of temples and shrines and on official palace seals and badges.

The Winged Solar Disc, and variations of it, are seen in many cultures. In Egypt it was called the Horus Behdety, and symbolized kingship, power, the flight of the soul and divinity. In Babylon, it was the symbol of the Sun God Utu/Shamash. The ancient Persian religion of Zoroastrianism revered it as the Faravahara, a symbol of Ahūra Mazda, the Supreme Being.

The Aten is a Sun Disc, originally an aspect of the God Ra in the traditional Egyptian pantheon. Pharaoh Akhenaten made the Aten into a monotheistic God – the sole focus of official worship from his capital city (and cult center) Amarna.

In Egyptian mythology, the Ibis-headed Thoth was the God of Wisdom, which included magic and writing. He was the keeper of his father's books and his library. He was also the god tasked with creating the different languages and scripts of mankind, after the Confusion of Tongues at the building of the Tower of Babel (before which, mankind practiced one religion and only spoke one language).

The ancient texts tell that the art of writing was taught to men by the gods, and across all ancient cultures this act has aways been seen as a magical gift from heaven, with the letters of the alphabet being among the most magical of all symbols as the building blocks of Creation, the foundation of cabala.

SIGILLAGRAPHIA

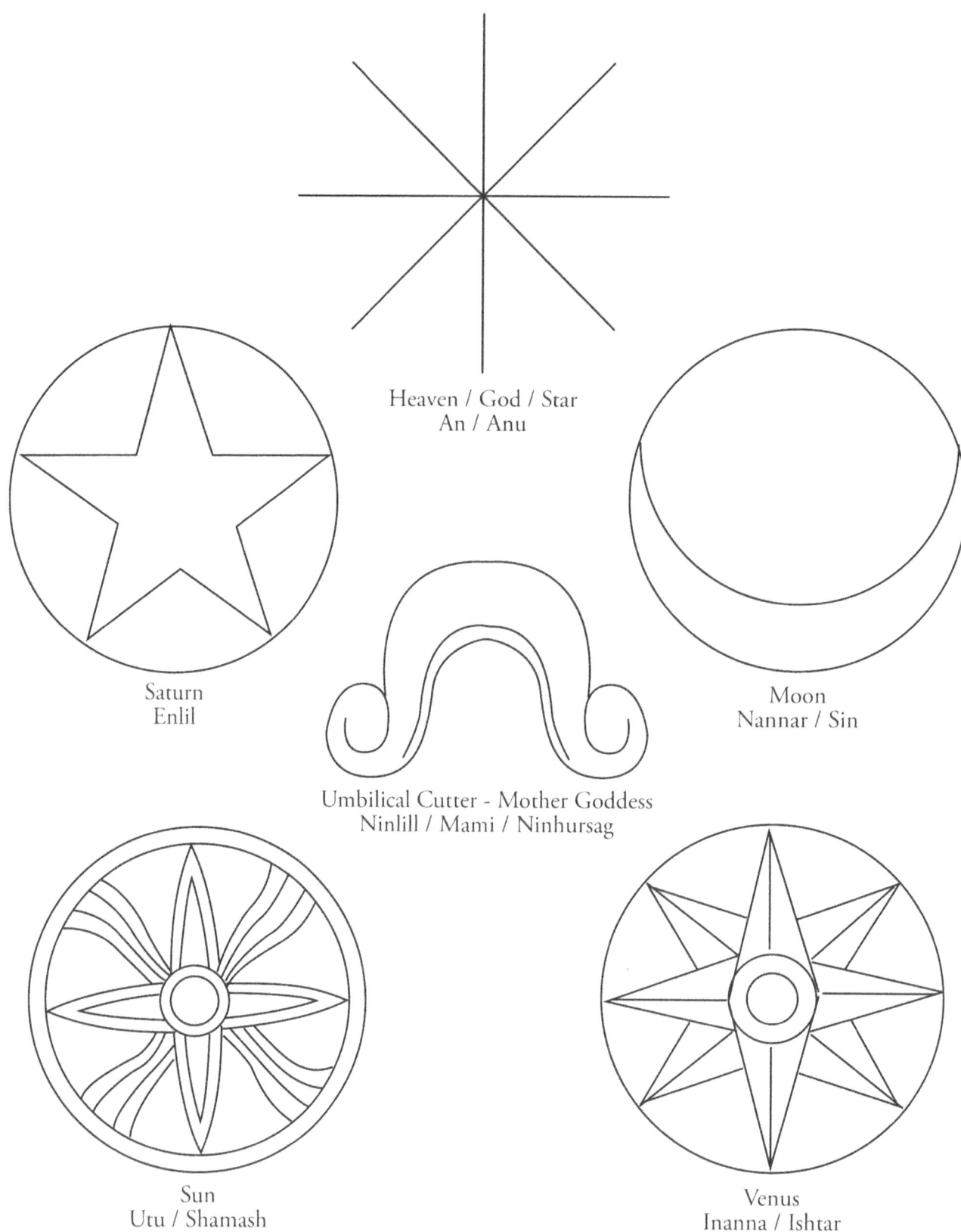

Seals of the Annunaki / Babylonian Sky Gods

ANCIENT WORLD

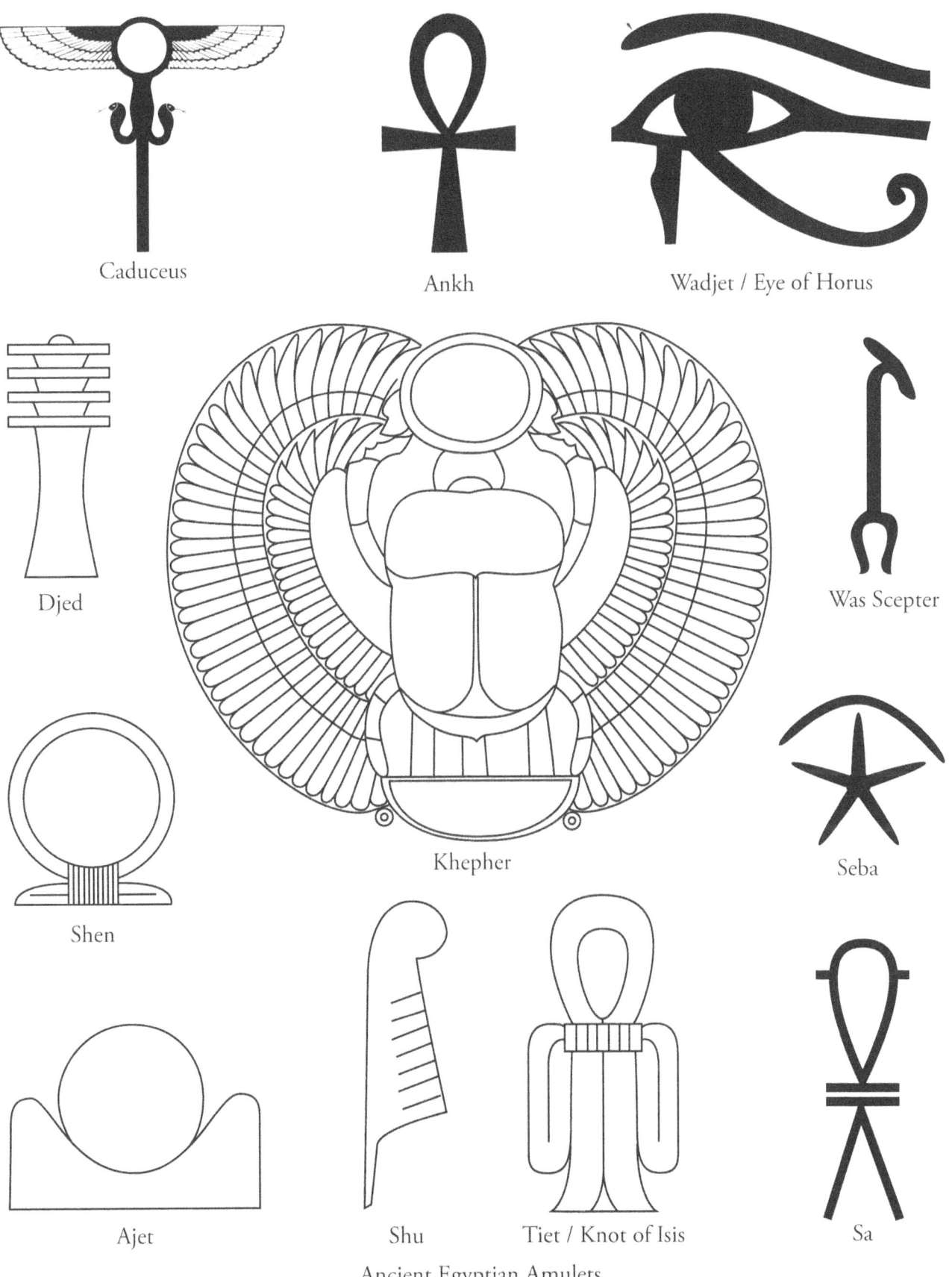

Ancient Egyptian Amulets

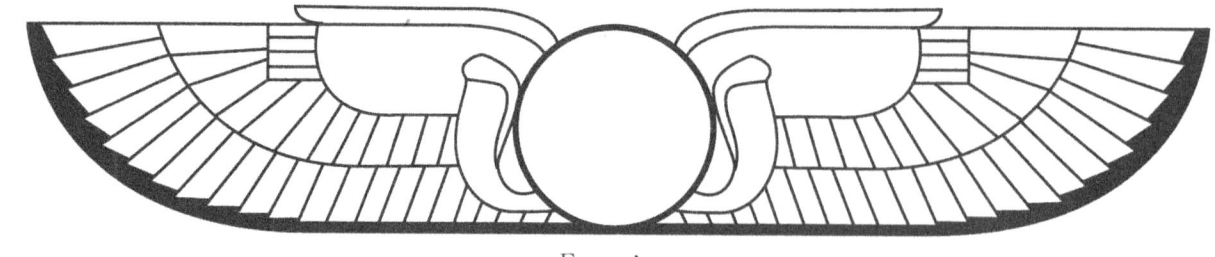
Egyptian

Assyrian

Farohar - Persian / Zoroastrian

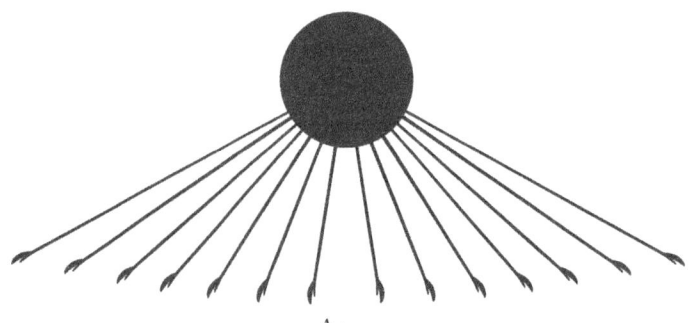
Aten

Winged Solar Disc

ANCIENT WORLD

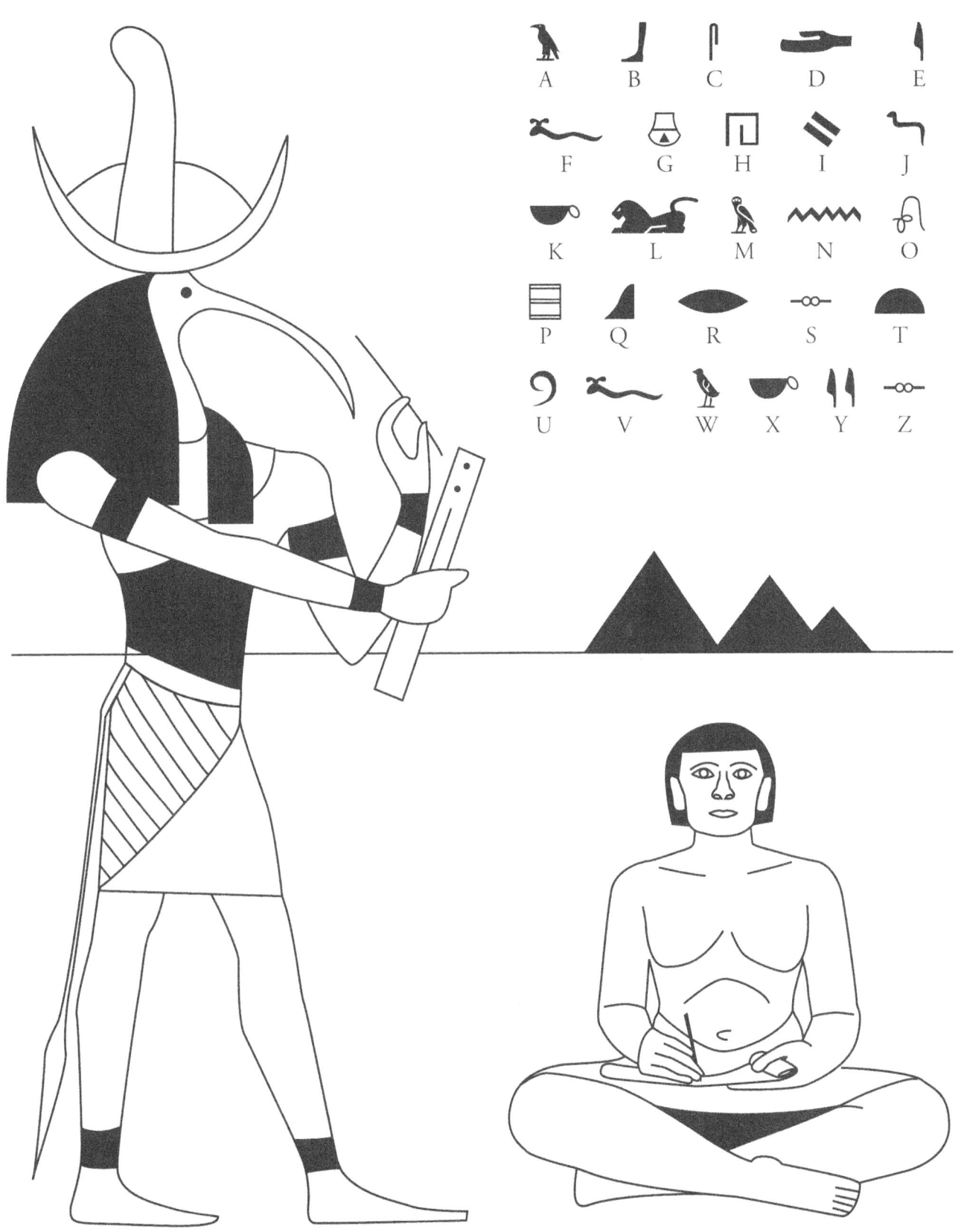

Egyptian Heiroglyphs for English

Classic World 1500 BCE–600 CE

The classic world centered around the eastern Mediterranean area of Egypt, Phoenicia, Greece, Palestine, Tunis and Rome.

Its early centuries saw the invention of the alphabet by the Phoenicians in 1050 BCE. Around 750 BCE, the Greeks adapted it to write Greek. Circa 550 BCE, Pythagoras used an archaic variant to express his Theory of Isopsephy, the numerological basis of cabala.

The dominant culture was Greek, with influences from the ancient Near East. It was the basis of European art, philosophy, society, education and magic.

The term 'magic' came into use during the Hellenic Era, from the Greek 'mageia' or 'magoi', derived from the Persian word 'Magi' – the title given to Zoroastrian priests.

Both Greeks and Romans believed magicians possessed arcane or secret knowledge and had the ability to channel power through polytheistic deities, spirits or ancestors of the ancient pantheon.

Greek authorities and officialdom used and also feared magic, and private individuals believed in magic. Farmers, with their dependency on the weather, wore amulets around their wrist or neck to guarantee rainfall.

Greek amulets fall into two categories: talismans, which brought good luck; and phylacteries, which protected. Amulets were made of wood, metal, stone and, more rarely, semi-precious stone.

They came in different shapes – miniature forms of the phallus, eye, vulva, knots, scarabs and obscene hand gestures – some of which are still widely used in Greece today, such as the Evil Eye.

The concept of the Evil Eye was widespread throughout the Mediterranean, with its roots in Greece. Coloured blue, the eye itself is believed to be derived from the eye of a bull and can be placed within the palm of the hand to enhance its protective power. Its meaning hasn't changed throughout the millennia.

The Caduceus, a very ancient symbol, is at least 4000 years old. As the emblem of the Greco-Roman God Hermes/Mercury, the rod or wand is the tool of all magicians, and is symbolic of the power and authority of magical and all supernatural forces.

The serpents remind us of hidden knowledge, forming an infinity symbol. The wings represent flight in physical and spiritual communication from heaven. The winged variant represents the Tree of Life. In the modern world, the wingless Caduceus is the emblem of the medical profession.

The Ouroboros is an ancient symbol that first appeared in Egypt around 1600 BCE, although it is likely much older. Named by the Greeks, it means 'Great Devourer' and speaks of motion, continuity and self-fertilization. It symbolizes not only the cyclical nature of time and the seasons, but also the eternal circle of rebirth and the eternity of Heaven and Earth working in harmony. In alchemy, it speaks of wholeness and infinity.

Hekate was a protective goddess who ruled over the earth, sea and sky, bestowing prosperity and daily blessings on families. Her symbol is a circular labyrinth, symbolizing rebirth, surrounding a center spiral symbolizing divine thought. Today, the symbol has been adopted by Greek Neopagans and the Dianic traditions of Wicca.

Saturn was the Roman God of Agriculture and Time. His festival, Saturnalia, was the feast of the winter solstice beginning on December 25th with the Feast of Sol Invicta (Mithras) and ending on January 1st with the Feast of Janus.

To celebrate Saturnalia, people decorated their homes with greenery and gave gifts of wax taper candles, called Cerei, signifying the light returning after the solstice.

Rome worshipped many religions and people of all classes paid a small fee to magicians trading outside temples for love potions, charms, spells and amulets. The Romans held a fear and ambivalence towards magic before they banned it.

In the classic world, the centre of learning was the Great Library of Alexandria in Ptolemaic Egypt. This mixing of ancient knowledge from India, Persia, Babylon and Egypt with existing

Hebrew and Greek mysticism influenced the creation of new esoteric movements, such as Gnosticism, Neoplatonism and Hermeticism, which contributed to the development of early Jewish and Christian mysticism.

Following the split of the Roman Empire and the rise of the Orthodox Church, books of magic were burned and the center of learning moved from Alexandria in Egypt to Arabia and Persia, where the last remains of Chaldean magic became incorporated into Sufic mystery.

The God Abraxas comes from Greco-Egyptian mysticism. He is a 'word spirit', higher than God and the Devil, who combines all opposites into One Being. He is associated with influencing many of the first Gnostics who had gone on to form the various Abrahamic religions, such as Judaism and Christianity.

The famous Abraxas talisman normally shows a man's body with the head of a cockerel, one arm with a shield and the other arm with a whip. He was engraved on gemstones used as amulets between the second and fourth centuries CE.

His magical name and its meaning are rooted in the secrecy of numerology, linked to the seven days of the week and the 365-day solar year.

On many of the magic amulets that were used against stomach diseases in the Greco-Roman period, the multi-rayed crown or nimbus was found, usually in connection with the lion or with leontocephaline figures like Mithras and Chnoubis.

Chnoubis, also named Yaldabaoth, is almost always depicted as being a man covered by a snake, serpent or dragon with a lion's head.

From ancient times, lions have been worshipped as animals of the Sun. The Jewish God Yahweh is also often depicted as a lion-faced anthropomorphic being who was Lord of Lightening, Thunder and Wind.

Mithraism was a potent religious force between the first and fourth centuries CE. Icons show Mithras fighting a bull and wearing a halo, the circular sign for a supernatural force.

Mithra was the Persian Sun God of Death and Resurrection, equivalent to the Egyptian Horus, the Greek Dionysus, the Syrian Adonis, Attis of Asia Minor and Jesus in Judea.

His cult spread as far as Greece and Rome where he was worshipped as Mithras, a god of light, truth and honour, with distinct differences between the Greek and Roman versions. His cult thrived in Rome as the legionnaire's god of choice.

Around the time of the birth of Jesus Christ, Greek, Coptic and Demotic scripts were frequently used to write some of the names of God—IAO, JAO, YAHWEH, JEHOVAH, SABAOTH, ADONAI—on magical papyri. These magical papyri contain early instances of the use of wands and other tools used in ceremonial magic.

Christianity began in the Middle East during the first century CE. By 500 CE, it had become the dominant religion of the Romanized areas of Asia, North Africa and Europe. The availability of the Septuagint ('Bible' written in Greek) was a major factor in the influence of Christianity among the literate.

Much of the foundation of Christian mysticism can be found in the pagan mystery religions of the ancient world. From the Babylonian myth of the Sun God Nimrod (Baal)—who married his mother Semiramis who, after his death, conceived his son Tammuz by immaculate conception—comes the belief of the Son of God conceived by a Holy Mother.

Its notion of a Supreme Being and Heaven and Hell are Zoroastrian in origin. The idea of a god of death and resurrection was widespread throughout the Mediterranean, North Africa and the Near East. In Egypt he was Horus; in Greece, Dionysus; in Syria, Adonis; in Persia he was Mithras; in Asia Minor he was Attis; and in Judea he was Jesus.

According to legend, many of the death and resurrection characters were born around the winter solstice to a virgin in humble surroundings with a star in the eastern sky. Some grew up to be spiritual masters with twelve disciples, performing miracles, giving baptisms and communion.

They all died, but only three of them – Horus, Mithras and Jesus – were crucified before experiencing a miraculous resurrection. A similar story can be found in the Odinic mysteries of the Norse, in the legends of Odin and his son Balder.

The Nimbus, or Halo, is an ancient sign of a supernatural being, associated with gods of death and resurrection. The Holy Trinity is represented by the Trefoils on the Eastern Crucifix.

SIGILLAGRAPHIA

Number	Sound	Name	Ancient Letter	Capital	Minuscule	Meaning
1	A	Alpha		A	α	cattle
2	B,	Beta		B	β	demon
3	G, J, Y	Gamma		Γ	γ	divinity
4	D	Delta		Δ	δ	fourfold
5	E	Epsilon		E	ε	ether
6	F	Diagamma	Ϝ ϛ			
7	Z	Zeta		Z	ζ	sacrifice
8	H	Eta		H	η	joy
9	Th	Theta		Θ	θ	crystal sphere
10	I	Iota		I	ι	destiny
20	K	Kappa		K	κ	illness
30	L	Lambda		Λ	λ	growth
40	M	Mu		M	μ	trees
50	N	Nu		N	ν	hag
60	Ks	Ksi		Ξ	ξ	fifteen stars
70	O	Omicron		O	ο	sun
80	P	Pi		Π	π	solar halo
90	W	Qoppa	ϟ ϙ			
100	R	Rho		P	ρ	fruitfulness
200	S	Sigma		Σ	σ	psycopomp
300	T	Tau		T	τ	human being
400	U, Y	Upsilon		Y	υ	flow
500	Ph, F	Phi		Φ	φ	phallus
600	Kh, X	Chi		X	χ	property
700	Ps	Psi		Ψ	ψ	heavenly light
800	OO	Omega		Ω	ω	abundance
900	SS	San/Sampi	ϻ Ↄ ϡ			

Greek Cabalistic Correspondences

CLASSIC WORLD

Letter	Sound	Planet	Greek God	Day	Note	Scale	Metal	Archangel	Colour	Direction
A	A	Moon	Hecate	Monday	A	si	silver	Michael	violet	East
E	E	Mercury	Hermes	Wednesday	E	mi	mercury	Gabriel	yellow	North
H	EE	Venus	Aphrodite	Friday	B	la	copper	Raphael	indigo	West
I	I	Sun	Apollo	Sunday	D	re	gold	Suriel	orange	South
O	O	Mars	Ares	Tuesday	C	do	iron	Raguel	red	Down
U	U	Jupiter	Zeus	Thursday	G	sol	tin	Anael	blue	Up
W	OU	Saturn	Kronos	Saturday	F	fa	lead	Saraphael	green	Centre

Vowel Correspondences

Letter	Element	Qualities	Greek God	Platonic Solid
G	Earth	cold and dry	Hades	cube
D	Water	cold and wet	Chronos	icosahedron
Q	Ether	all	Zeus	dodecahedron
P	Fire	hot and dry	Ares	tetrahedon
R	Air	hot and wet	Dionysus	octahedron

Letters of the Elements

Letter	Zodiac Sign	Month
B	Aries	March-April
Z	Taurus	April-May
K	Gemini	May-June
L	Cancer	June-July
M	Leo	July-August
N	Virgo	August-September
X	Libra	September-October
S	Scorpio	October-November
T	Sagittarius	November-December
F	Capricorn	December-January
C	Aquarius	January-Febuary
Y	Pisces	Febuary-March

Twelve Signs of the Zodiac and the Months of the Year

Tables of Correspondence

SIGILLAGRAPHIA

Ouroborous

Matiasma - Evil Eye

Hecate's Wheel

Hercule's Knot

Saturnalia

Mithras / Sol Invicta

Caduceus

Halo / Nimbus

Greco-Roman Symbols

CLASSIC WORLD

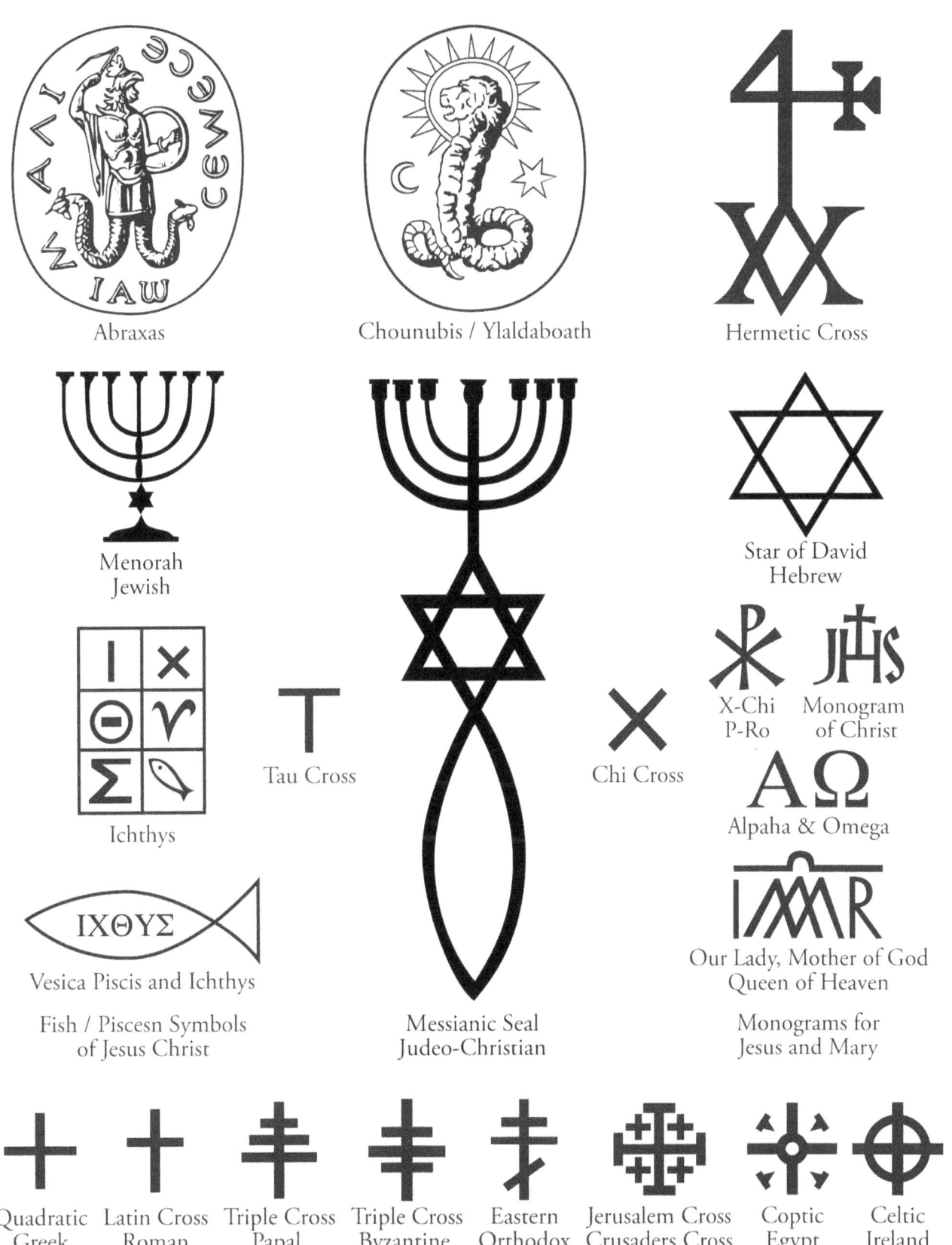

Gnostic, Hermetic, Jewish and Early Christian Symbols

SIGILLAGRAPHIA

30

Medieval and Renaissance World 600–1600

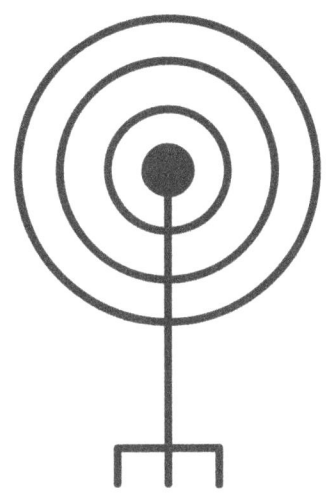

Medieval World 600–1450

During the European conversion to Christianity, 300–1100 CE, pagan magic became synchronized with Christian dogma, in which magic was strictly identified with paganism. Many early Christians condemned magic practice, which they associated with the pagan traditions of Greco-Roman society. For them, magic was taught by demons and worked through the power of demons. This tradition carried on into the Medieval and Renaissance worlds.

In the period between 1022 and 1850, the Roman Church systematically demonized the non-Christian beliefs of Europe. The result was a charge of heresy for witches, pagans, gnostics, alchemists, magicians, sorcerers and others, leading to the genocide of the Cathars, the Inquisition, witch-burning and magic symbols being associated solely with black magic.

This demonization of the non-Christian beliefs and practices of witches, pagans and gnostics continued until the twentieth century and played a pivotal role in the rise of neopaganism.

Generally, the Medieval Era is divided into three periods—Early, High and Late—and is referred to as the Middle Ages. Renaissance scholars referred to the whole of the Middle Ages as the Dark Ages, because they perceived it to be devoid of intellectual enlightenment. Today, the term Dark Ages is used to refer to the Early period only.

In the Early period, 500–1000, medicinal practices were often regarded as forms of natural magic. Prayers, blessings and exorcisms were all common forms of verbal formulas whose intentions were hard to distinguish between the magical and the religious.

This led to difficulty in distinguishing between helpful 'white' magic and unhelpful 'black' magic. Medical magic and protective magic were regarded as helpful magic, while sorcery was considered black magic and evil. Magic was only punished if it was deemed to be done with harmful intention, which made it black magic.

In 711, the Muslim Moor's of North Africa conquered Spain and began an expansion of literature into magical instruction that peaked in the twelfth and thirteenth centuries. This interaction between Christians and Muslims resulted in the translation of astrological and magical learning, which had been preserved in Arabic, Hebrew and Greek, into Latin, enabling the concept of magic to be further developed during the High and Late periods.

The High Medieval period, 1000–1350, is seen to typify the Middle Ages, as represented by the Crusades. The Knights Templar were a Christian military order, founded in 1118, with their headquarters on the Temple Mount in Jerusalem until 1128. The order was active until 1312, when it was permanently suppressed by Pope Clement V.

Over the centuries, they have become associated with legends concerning secrets and mysteries handed down to the select from ancient times – obtained from Christian, Jewish, Arabic, Hermetic and Gnostic sources.

Associated with the Holy Grail and the Ark of the Covenant, they were historically accused of witchcraft for the idolic worship of Baphomet, a secret name for Mohammed.

From the beginning of the High Medieval Era, the Western occult tradition is ultimately derived from the Hellenistic magic of Hermeticism, which absorbed Arabic alchemy and astrology and Jewish cabalistic mysticism. This was strengthened in the seventeenth century by the Rosicrucians and their brand of spiritual alchemy that survived the Enlightenment.

Translated in the twelfth century from Arabic and Greek into Latin, the Hermetica is a set of philosophical, religious and esoteric beliefs based primarily on the writings of Hermes Trismegistus, or Thrice Great Hermes. The Thrice Great refers to Thoth, Hermes and Mercury; the composite Hermes – hence the term Hermetica: the foundation of astrology, alchemy and Sacred Geometry.

Hermetica is generally traced back to the Greco-Egyptian city of Alexandria. The movement unified elements of Jewish and Christian mysticism with Greek Platonism and Egyptian occult beliefs (Osiris, Isis, Horus). The resulting composite proved compelling to medieval Islamic and Christian scholars, and to the later intellectuals of the Renaissance.

Hermeticism was seen as being opposed to the Christian Church. It became part of the occult underworld, intermingling with other occult movements and practices. It was rediscovered at the beginning of the Renaissance as a lost text called the Corpus Hermeticum.

Possibly the most famous Hermetic work is a short scientific text called the Emerald Tablet. It was paramount in influencing Isaac Newton in the area of matter theory, since alchemy concerns itself with the various manifestations and transformations of matter (lead into gold, etc). It is also the first text to espouse the well-known occult maxim, 'As above, so below'. The Smaragdina Tablet is a medieval pictorial interpretation of the original text.

Over the centuries, secrecy has hidden the number of groups associated with Hemeticism. Rosicrucianism was a Hermetical Christian movement dating back to the fifteenth century and believed to have ceased in the nineteenth century, though some say it fell into complete secrecy.

The Hermetic Order of the Golden Dawn was specifically a hermetic society, teaching the arts of alchemy, cabala and hermetic magic, along with the principles of occult science.

Alchemy was the great magical work created by Hermes Trismegistus, the founder of the arts and sciences. In the ancient world, 'alkhemy' was the secret art of the Land of Khem – the ancient Egyptian name for Egypt, the home of Thoth. The 'Al' preceding 'Khem' is Arabic.

Alchemy's most familiar symbol is the Philosopher's Stone, a mystical diagram used to achieve the prime principle of alchemy – turning lead into gold, both physically and spiritually.

The most common alchemical sigils are those of the four elements—air, water, fire and earth—which play an important part in all mysticism. The most pertinent symbols of the alchemical spirits include the three philosophical signs: sulphur, salt and mercury. Related to these signs are the seven metalloids: vitriol, saltpetre, gal ammonia, alum, sulphur, salt and antimony.

Although some of the alchemical symbols occasionally varied a little between practitioners, the meanings of the simpler symbols are so universal that they extend well beyond the reaches of this one system.

The most famous work of Arabic astrological magic was a compilation known as the Picatrix, which explained how to conjure the spirits associated with the planets, how to inscribe images of the heavenly bodies on metal and the use of magical procedures.

The medieval magicians of the twelfth century also drew on Jewish traditions for inspiration. Cabalistic works held a long Jewish tradition of gaining knowledge through magical contact with angels and the power found in Hebrew words.

Jewish cabala emerged suddenly in Southwest France and Spain between 1174 and 1200, at a time when cabala reached a pinnacle of importance for Judaism in medieval Europe.

The earliest Jewish cabalistic work, the Sefer Yetzirah, or Book of Creation, was written in the second century CE. It sets out each of the 22 letters of the Hebrew alphabet as a symbol with specific meanings, and correspondences to its teachings are found in the texts of related writings called the Sefer Zohar, or Book of Splendor, written around 1280.

With this knowledge, cabalistic mystics seek to bridge the abyss between man and God through the symbolism of the sephiroth and religious observances. Modern cabala is based on the Sefer Zohar as interpreted by the Hermetic Order of the Golden Dawn in the nineteenth century.

The Late Medieval period, 1350–1450, is renowned for the Black Death. At this time, magic was regarded as part of a widespread and dangerously anti-social, demonic cult, leading to the persecution of witches and magicians for practising black magic, while forms of white magic persisted in Europe. Practices such as medical magic, astrology, alchemy, charms and sorcery dated back centuries before they were considered evil.

The Catholic Church condemned such practices in about 800. But it was not until the publication of the Malleus Maleficarum in Germany, by Catholic clergyman Heinrich Kramer in 1487, that individuals who practiced things that were considered witchcraft and sorcery were punished severely.

Written in Latin, the title roughly translates as "Hammer of the Witches". It was essentially a guide on how to convict an individual of witchcraft. Kramer made a specific connection between women and satanic magic that became widespread.

SIGILLAGRAPHIA

Thoth

As Above,
So Below

Essence
Life

Mercury

Emerald Tablet (Phoenician script)

Smaragdina Tablet
Hermetica

Hermes

Quintessence
Ether / 5th Element

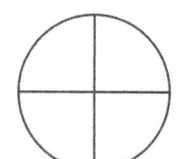
Universal Seed
Creation

Hermes Trismegistus

34

MEDIEVAL WORLD

Mercury - Spirit   Salt - Body   Sulphur - Soul

3 Primes

Air — wind, warmth, Holy Spirit, breath

Water — female, intuition, moist, cold, Baptisms

Earth — material, movement, physical sensations, cool, dark

Fire — male, light, love, passion, hate, anger, moving energy to reach the divine

Four Elements and the Philosopher's Stone

Antimony   Arsenic   Bismuth   Boron   Lithium   Magnesium

Phosphorus   Platinum   Potassium   Sulphur   Zinc

Mundane Elements

Amalgam   Aqua Fortis   Aqua Regia   Aqua Vitae   Cinnabar   Sal Ammoniac   Vitriol

Compound Elements

Alchemy

SIGILLAGRAPHIA

Saturn - Lead

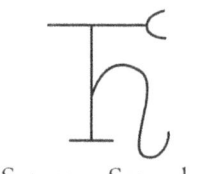
Saturn - Saturday

Saturn

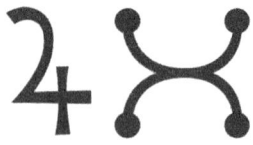
Jupiter - Tin

Jupiter - Wednesday

Jupiter

Mars - Iron

Mars - Tuesday

Mars

Sun - Gold

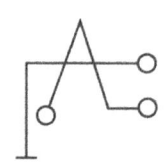
Sun - Sunday

Sun

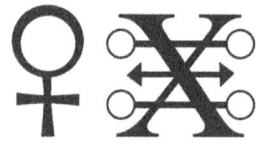
Venus - Copper

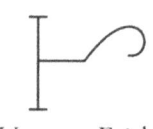
Venus - Friday

Venus

Mercury (Quicksilver)

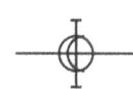
Mercury - Thursday

Mercury

Moon - Silver
Planetary Metals

Moon - Monday
Planetary Sigils

Moon
Planetary Characters

Planetary Metals and Characters

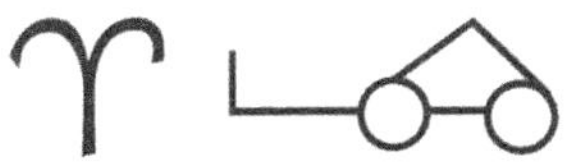

MEDIEVAL WORLD

Aries - Calcination

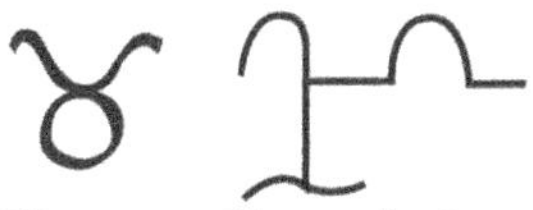

Taurus - Congelation

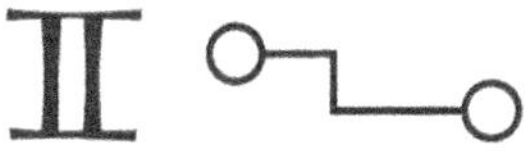

Gemini - Fixation

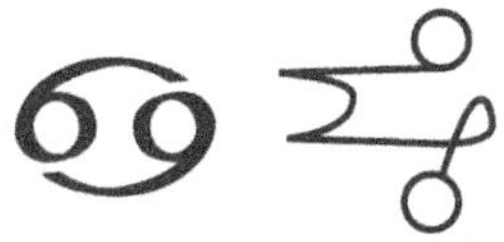

Cancer - Dissolution

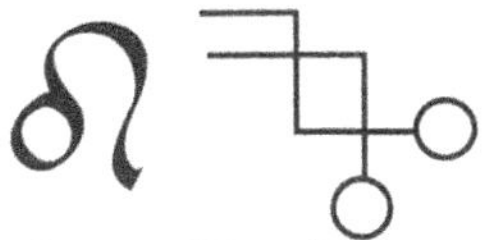

Leo - Dissolution

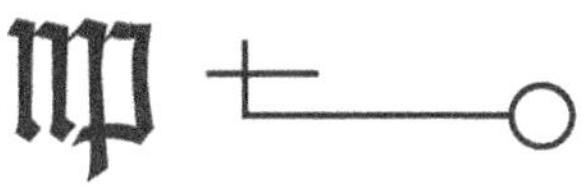

Virgo - Distillation

Western or Tropical Zodiac (Solar)
Center Out - Monad, New Moons, 12 Pointed Star/Sun,
Ruling Planets, Constellations, Astrological Signs, Names

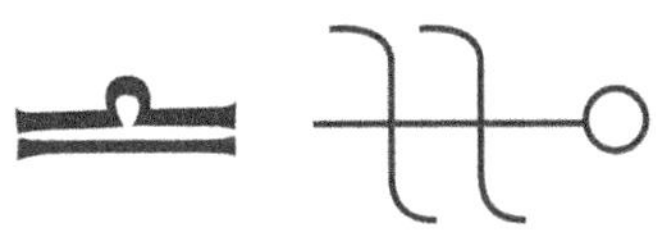

Libra - Sublimination

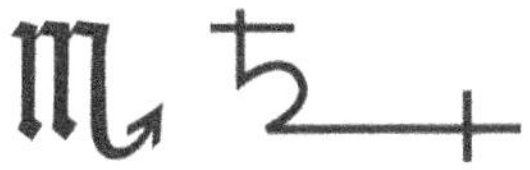

Scorpio - Separation

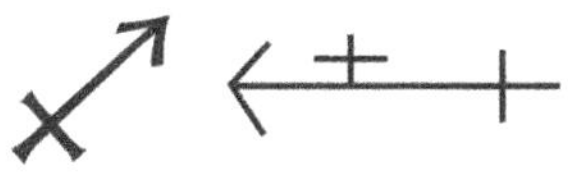

Sagittarius - Ceration

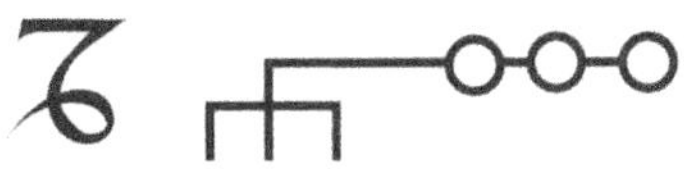

Capricorn - Fermentation (Putrefaction)

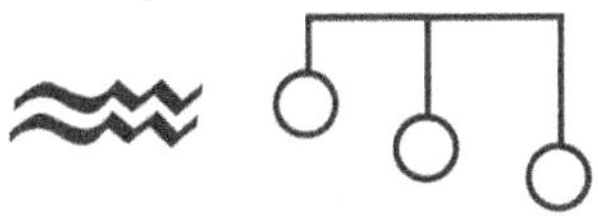

Aquarius - Multiplication

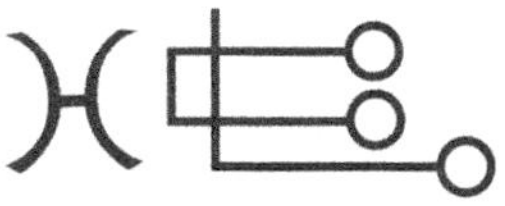

Pisces - Projection

As Ciphers for Chemical Operations

Astrological Signs

SIGILLAGRAPHIA

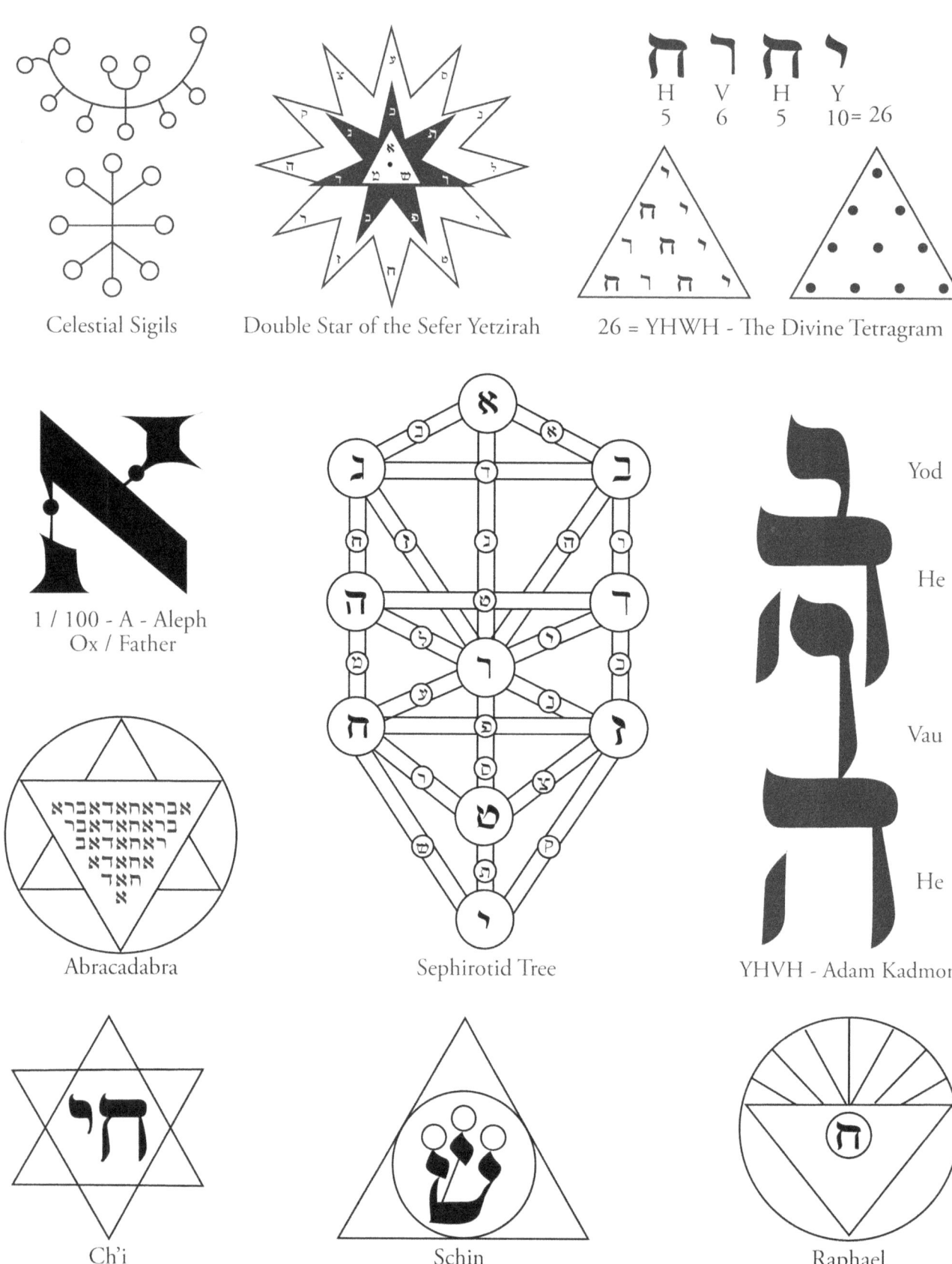

Celestial Sigils

Double Star of the Sefer Yetzirah

26 = YHWH - The Divine Tetragram

1 / 100 - A - Aleph
Ox / Father

Abracadabra

Sephirotid Tree

YHVH - Adam Kadmon

Ch'i

Schin
Jewish Cabalis

Raphael

MEDIEVAL WORLD

Number Value	Hebrew Letter	Letter Sound	Hebrew Name	Name Meaning	Tarot Card Equivalent
1/100	א	A	Aleph	ox	Fool
2	ב	B	Beth	house	Magician
3	ג	G	Gimmel	camel	Empress
4	ד	D	Daleth	door	Emperor
5	ה	H	He	window	Heirophant
6	ו	V/W	Vau/Waw	hook	Lovers
7	ז	Z	Zayin	sword	
8	ח	Ch	Cheth	fence	Chariot
9	ט	Th	Teth	serpent	Strength
10	י	Y/I/J	Yod	hand	Hermit
20/500	כ ך	K	Kaph	palm of hand	Wheel of Fortune
30	ל	L	Lamed	ox goad	Justice
40/600	מ ם	M	Mem	water	Hanged Man
50/700	נ ן	N	Nun	fish	Death
60	ס	X/SS	Samekh	support	Temperance
70	ע	O	Ayin	eye	Devil
80/800	פ ף	P	Pe	mouth	Tower
90/900	צ ץ	Tz	Tzaddi	fish hook	Star
100	ק	Q	Qoph	back of head	Moon
200	ר	R	Resh	head	Sun
300	ש	Sh	Shin	tooth-flame	Judgement
400	ת	T	Tau	sign	World

Hebrew Cabalistic Correspondences

Renaissance 1450–1600

From the beginning of the Late Medieval Era around 1250 to the end of the Renaissance, circa 1600, Christian mysticism mixed with Hermeticism, alchemy, arabic astrology, Jewish mysticism and necromancy, giving rise to the first grimoires and the scholarly occultism that evolved into the High Magic of European occultism.

Its primary concern was the ritual and ceremonies used in the conjuration of spirits by the magician. This is the form of magic that the modern mind associates with black magic.

The High Magic of Europe also owes much to Babylonian and Chaldean magic as the precursor of early European medieval magic. This is instanced not only by the similarities of the systems, but also by the introduction into medieval magic of Chaldean gods and magicians.

The Babylonian names of demons, such as Beelzebub, Astaroth (Ishtar/Astarte), Baal and Moloch appeared along with allusions to 'wise men' and the 'Necromancers of Babylon', 'Star Gazers of Chaldea' and the Witch Goddess Lilith. These gods were appealed to more frequently than those of the Egyptians.

Apart from practising sorcery, witchcraft and folk magic, it became fashionable to write anything connected with magic in one or more of the dead scripts from the ancient and classic worlds, particularly Egyptian hieroglyphs and Hebrew and Greek characters. Because of their antiquity, these scripts were considered to be holders of great magical power and resonance.

Because more people were becoming literate in Latin, they were used as ciphers to hide the esoteric knowledge condemned by the Christian Church (although the majority of magicians considered themselves essentially Christian).

In the Renaissance, the invocation of spirits using ritual magic was the focus of much occult practice, resulting in the publication of magical training books called grimoires that contained conjurations and renditions of the sigils, seals and pentacles thought to be useful when invoking spirits.

The astrological magic of the medieval world was sometimes referred to as necromancy. But in the Late Middle Ages and Renaissance, the most troubling form of magic became necromancy, or talking with the dead. Those involved were mainly practiced men who were educated as the ability to read, write and speak Latin was required.

Necromancy originally meant 'summoning the spirits of the deceased'. But, at the time, the terms 'necromantia' or 'necromancy', and 'nigormantia' or 'black magic', were fundamentally interchangeable – leading to much confusion.

This led to a rise in sorcery trials in the fourteenth century, with those at the end of the fifteenth century being the most dramatic – the sorcery of an individual who acted with other witches on behalf of the Devil. Another reason for the rise in frequency of trials was the change from parchment to paper, to record information more cheaply.

Judeo-Christian mysticism had a long tradition of invoking both God and his angels for assistance and knowledge. Christianity drew on the beneficent divine power of God, archangels and angels – all other rites drew on the necessary evil force of demons. Magicians, by the very performance of their arts, entered into pacts with demons and so became agents of the devil.

There are different types of spirit for the conjurer to call upon. These entities can be classified into groups depending on their status, and invoked for different reasons due to the nature of the spirit. They include planetary spirits, elemental spirits, Olympic spirits, sephirotic and celestial spirits, archangels, angels, demons and others.

Archangels are the chief angels, or first in rank, and act as messengers or envoys. The system of twelve archangels corresponds to the signs of the zodiac. The system of seven archangels corresponds to the seven planets, seven days of the week, seven colours of the rainbow and seven notes on the musical scale, as well as having other properties.

As well as their Hebrew names, there are also Christian and Islamic variants, leading to a divergence of correspondence among them.

Sephirotic angels are forces that send

information and sensation between mankind and the Tetragrammaton, or YHWH. Because of this, it is reasoned that they should not be worshipped, prayed to, nor invoked. When they appear they are seen only from the viewpoint of the recipient, which will be anthropomorphic.

In the ceremonial magic of King Solomon, the 72 angels of the Shemhamphorash protect the conjuror from the 72 demons they are numerically paired with. Each angel controls and counters a specific demon, typically of the same number.

There is a discrepancy in this number system, so it doesn't directly match up, and their names and sigils vary from grimoire to grimoire, even though they are essentially the same 'Enochic' demons.

Belief in demons goes back many millennia. Zoroastrianism teaches that there are 3,333 demons, some with specific dark responsibilities such as war, starvation, sickness, etc.

Some believe these concepts are received as part of the cabalistic tradition. Others perceive that demons were part of healing magic used to describe medical conditions such as epilepsy and mental illnesses.

Some scholars suggest that the origin of early demonology can be traced to two distinct mythologies of evil – Adam and Enoch. The Adamic story traces the source of evil to Satan's transgression and the Fall of Man. The Enochic tradition bases its demons on the names of the Fallen Angels, led by Azazel, listed against their transgressions, as recorded in the Book of Enoch.

The ranks given to the spirits—Duke, Marquis, Count and Knight—are European in origin. High-ranking demons like Lucifer, Astaroth, Baal, Leviathan, Beelzebub and Behemoth were fashioned as the Dukes of Hell with their own infernal hordes or servitors.

The Renaissance was a pinnacle of European culture not only in art and sculpture, but also in the sciences, and many influential manuscripts were produced during this era. A scholarly work of Medieval and Renaissance High Magic was published in 1533 by Heinrich Cornelius Agrippa, titled The Three Books of Occult Philosophy.

He recorded how geomantic characters, magic ciphers, planetary kamea, sacred names and rituals could be used to magical effect. Like the Pseudomonarchia Daemonum and the Lesser Keys of Solomon, Agrippa also explains how demons may be conjured and commanded, although he warns that the magician must do this with the aid of good spirits or angels.

For the most part, the literature of magical instruction was either written anonymously or pseudonymously – like the works ascribed to King Solomon or, from 1480 onwards, those writings from antiquity ascribed to the mythological Hermes Trimegistus.

Manuscripts ascribed to the Biblical King Solomon date from early antiquity in Arabic, but appear in Hebrew and Greek in the thirteenth and fourteenth centuries, and Italian in the sixteenth and seventeenth centuries, with English versions in the nineteenth century.

In the legend, King Solomon was given a magic ring by the Archangel Michael to compel the 72 Princes of Hell to build him a temple, before he bound them in a vessel of brass.

His most famous works are the sixteenth century Keys of Solomon, containing the Holy Pentacles, and the seventeenth century Lesser Keys of Solomon, concerning the conjuration of demons.

The Enochian magic of Dr John Dee and Edward Kelley was a unique form of Renaissance angelic magic from Elizabethan England. Dee and Kelley used a method called 'scrying', or looking into a magic mirror within which the angels revealed their knowledge.

They began with the Seal of Ameth to divine the names of angelic spirits. Next, the angels gave them an angelic language and script, supposedly last spoken by the biblical Enoch (hence Enochian magic). They also received a great number of magic tables, including the Great Table – a map of the Universe containing the hidden names and sigils of the 91 Governors.

At the advice of the angels, Dee and Kelley never practiced Enochian magic and, like the Keys of Solomon, it lay forgotten in the British Library until revised into its modern form by the Hermetic Order of the Golden Dawn in the late nineteenth century.

SIGILLAGRAPHIA

Michael - Sunday | Gabriel - Monday | Samuel - Tuesday | Raphiel - Wednesday

Angels of the Days of the Week - The Magus

Mephgazub
Mogarip
Amabosar
Black Venus Angels

Angel Belvaspata

Archangel Micheal

Och
Bethor
Belzazel
Olympic Angels

Raphael Archangel Tipharech Sun | Gabriel Archangel Yesod Moon | Michael Archangel Hod Mercury

Abametra/Venus
Cornifex/Mars
Paymon/Mercury
Planetary Angels

Raziel Archangel Chokmah Neptune | Metatron Archangel Kethor Uranus | Sanfalphom Archangel Malkuth

Sephirotic Angels

Sachiel Zadkiel Anathiel
Anael Samuel
Celestial Archangels Sefer Yetzirah

Hahaiah | Iezale | Mebahel | Harie | Yeiayel (Ieiael) | Lanoiah | Caliel | Leuviah

Angels of the Shemhamphorash

Angelic Spirits and Sigil Styles

42

RENAISSANCE

Astaroth

Beelzebub

Lucifer

Seals of the Dukes of Hell - Grimorium Verum

MURIEL
Great Demon of Lies

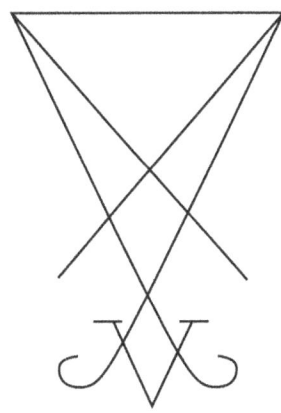

PAIMON
Master of Infernal Ceremonies

MEPHISTOPH
Lord of the Host

Sigil of Lucifer - Grimorium Verum

ZEPAR
Deforms the Unborn

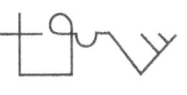

CAMAEL
The Destroyer

Agrippa's Demons

Signature of Leviathan

SYTRI
Lord of Luxury

Solomon's Demons

Seal of Lilith

Red King / Sulpher (Behemoth)

Seal of Astaroth (Goetic)

Demonic Spirits and Sigil Styles

Judaeo-Christian

Christian

Islam

6th Book of Moses - Spirit of Fire

7th Book of Moses - Spirit of Fire

Cabalistic

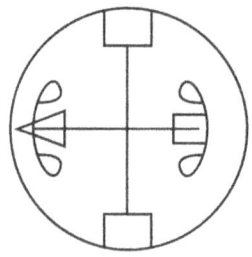
Greek 14th c,
Solomonic Seal Variants

Hebrew 15th c.

Seals of Archangels
Graphic Variation of Seal Design

RENAISSANCE

Seals of the Sages of the Pyrimid - Black Proof Grimoire

SIGILLAGRAPHIA

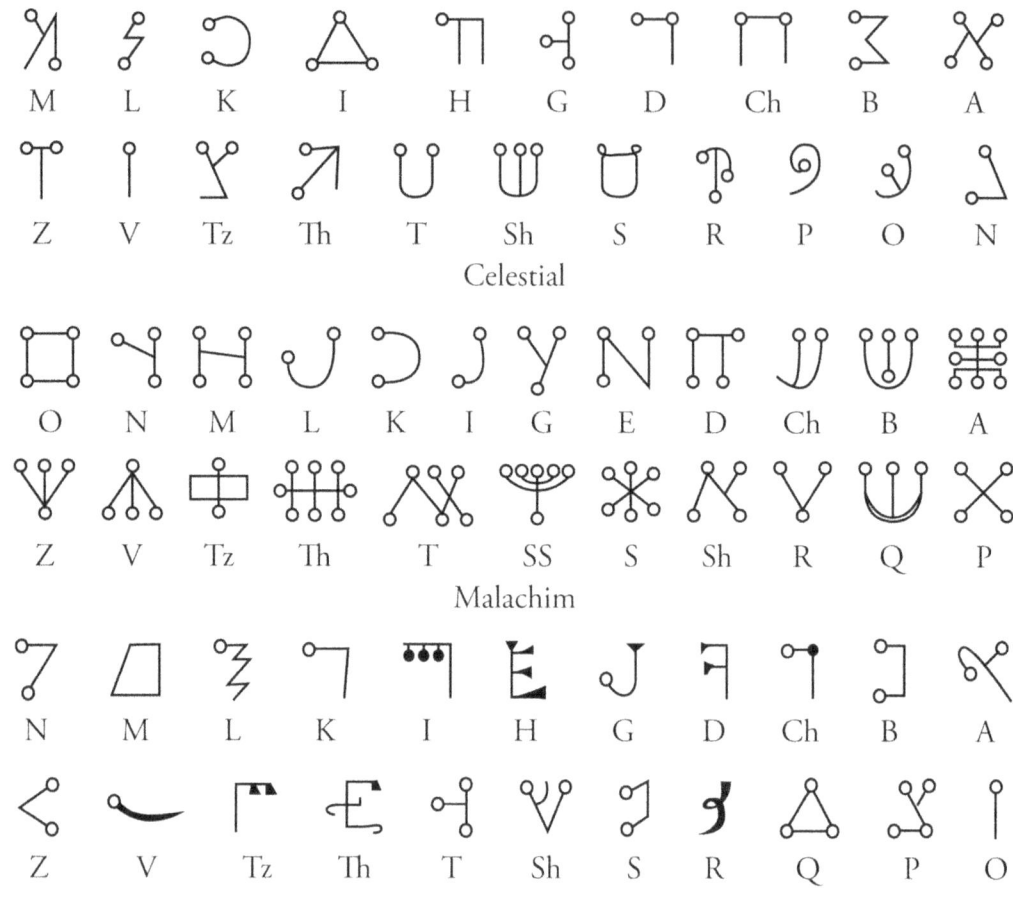

Tranitus Fluvi / Passing the River Script

Celsestial / Angelic Cipher Scripts for Writing Hebrew

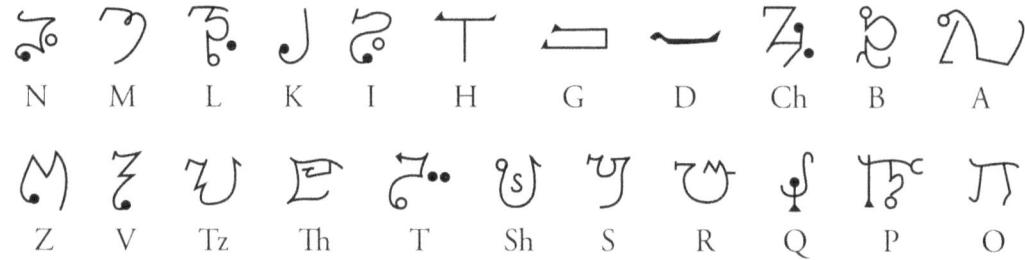

Writing of the Magi - Cipher Script for the Hebrew Names of Angels Written on Seals and Pentacles

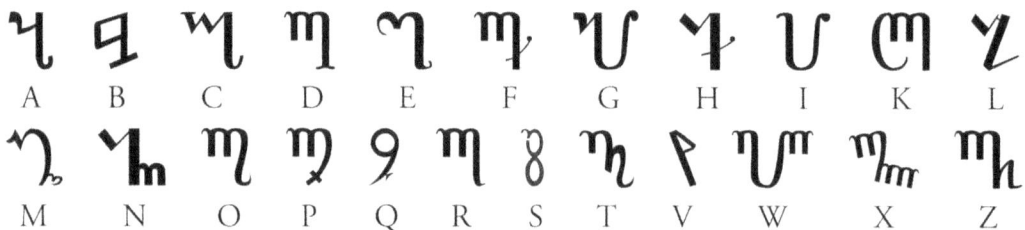

Theban / Runes of Honourius / Witche's Alphabet - Cipher Script for Latin

Cipher Scripts for Hebrew and Latin - H C Agrippa

RENAISSANCE

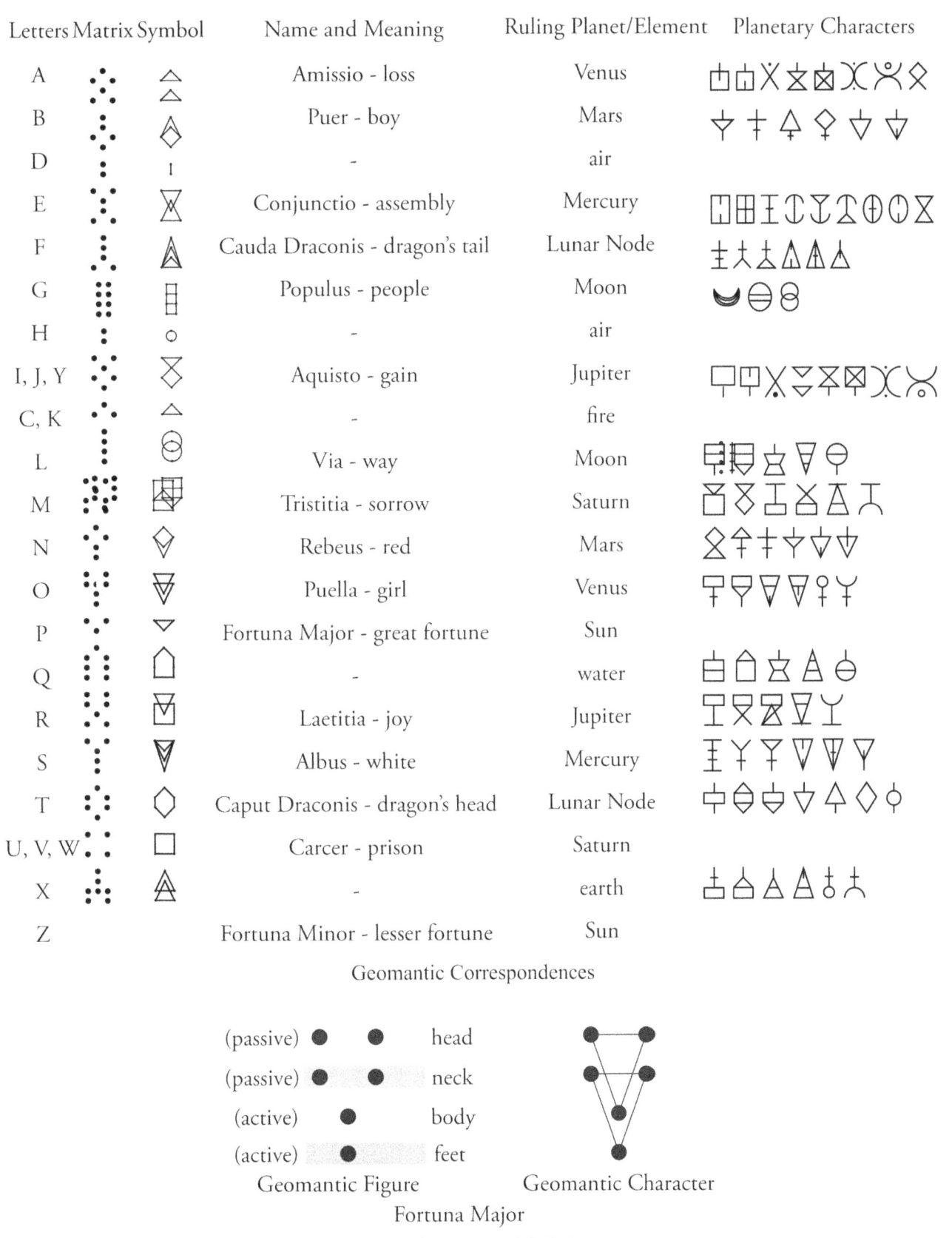

Geomantic Correspondences

Geomantic Figure — Fortuna Major

Geomantic Character

Geomantic Characters - H C Agrippa

SIGILLAGRAPHIA

Aiq Bkr / Nine Chambers Cipher - H C Agrippa

RENAISSANCE

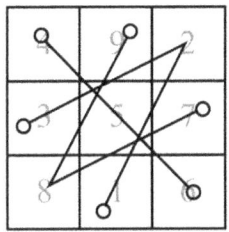

Seal of Saturn
Kameas 3x3 magic constant 15
total (3x15) 45

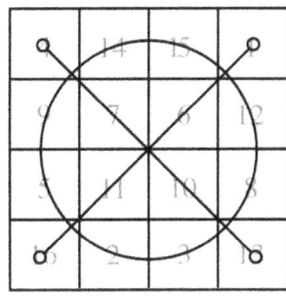

Seal of Jupiter
Kameas 4x4 magic constant 34
total (4x34) 136

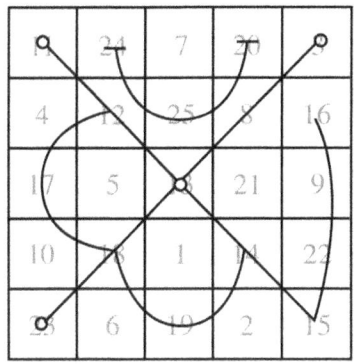

Seal of Mars
Kameas 5x5 magic constant 65
total (5x65) 325

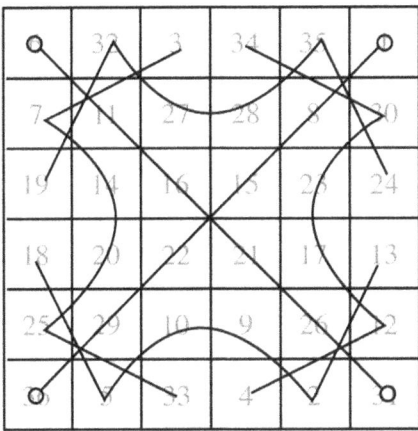

Seal of the Sun
Kameas 6x6 magic constant 111
total (6x111) 666

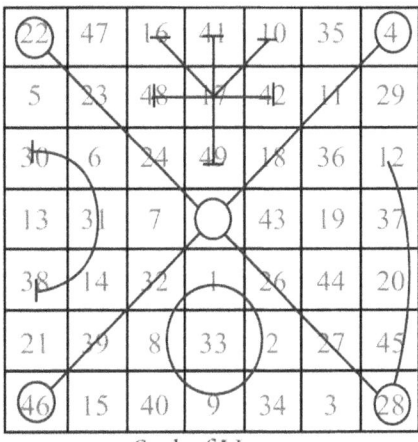

Seal of Venus
Kameas 7x7 magic constant 175
total (7x175) 1225

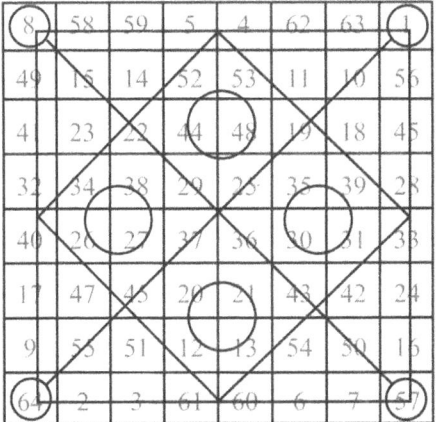

Seal of Mercury
Kameas 8x8 magic constant 64
total (8x64) 2080

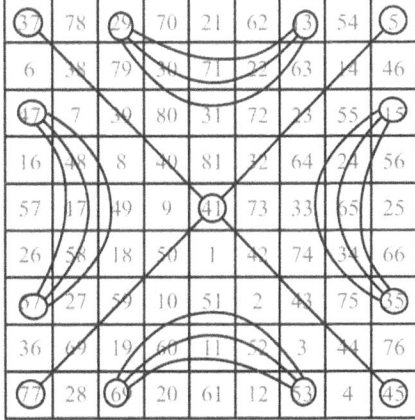

Seal of the Moon
Kameas 9x9 magic constant 369
total (9x369) 3321

(Magic Squares) Planetary Kamea and their Seals - H C Agrippa

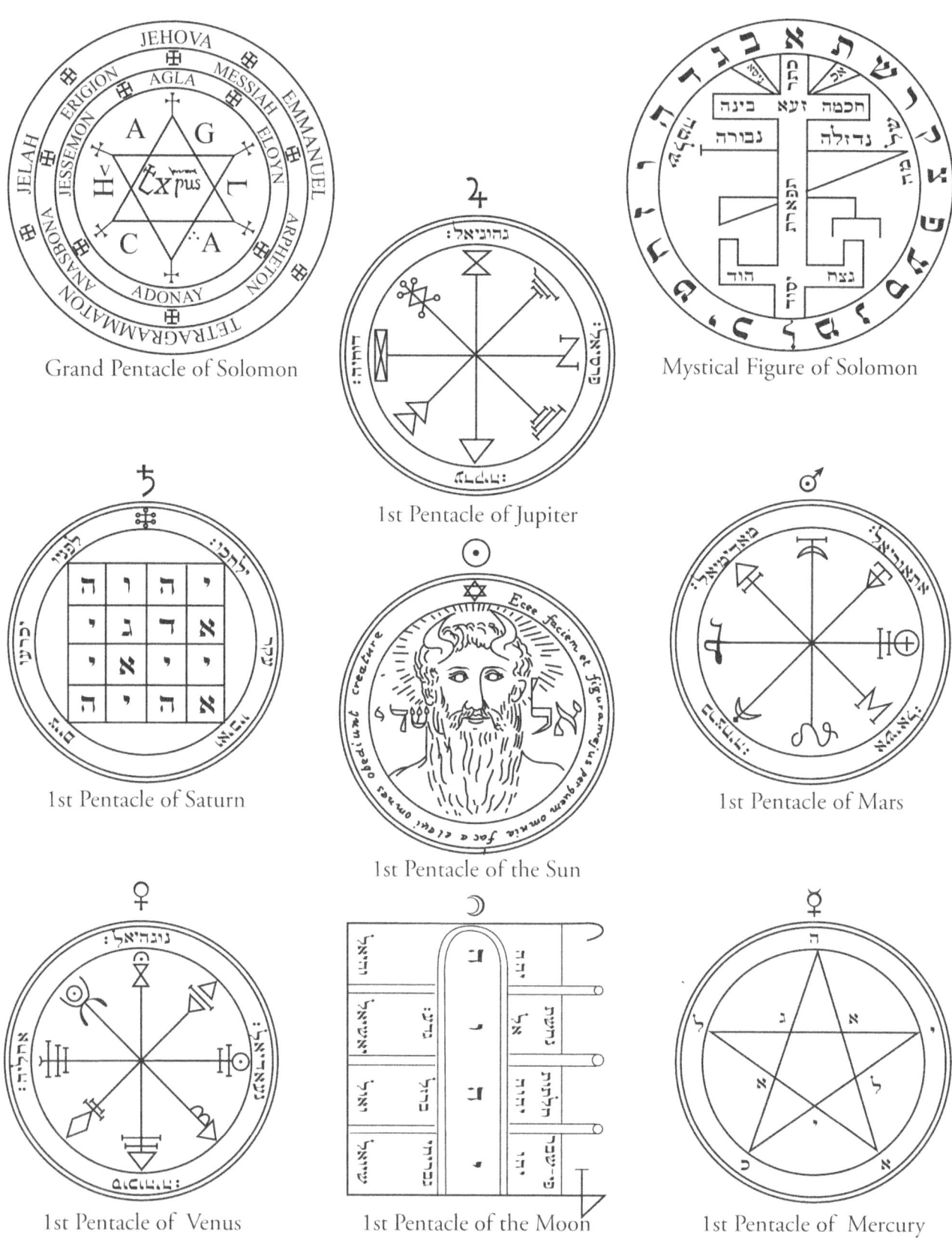

Holy Pentacles / Planetary Medals - Keys of Solomon

RENAISSANCE

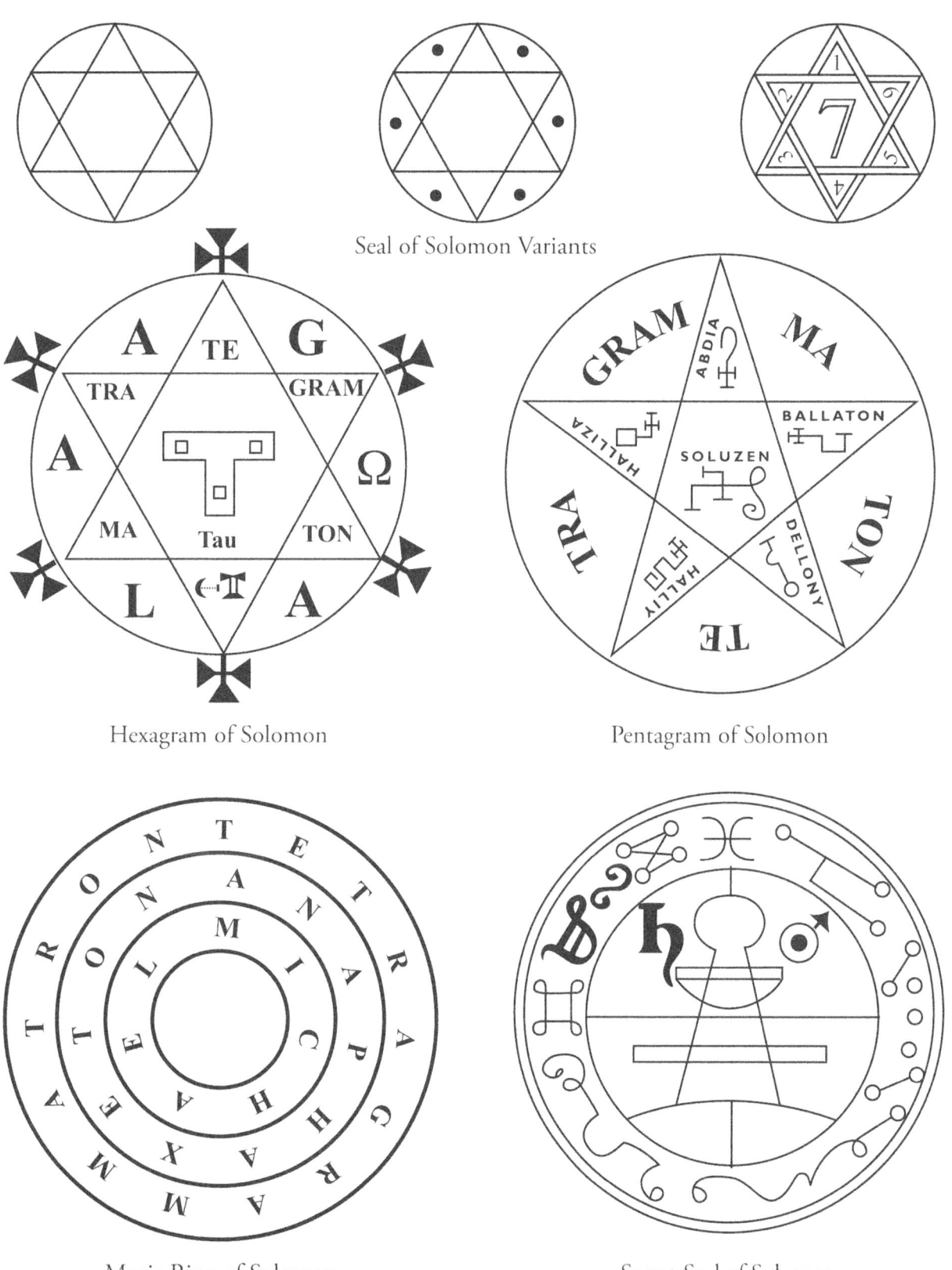

Seal of Solomon Variants

Hexagram of Solomon

Pentagram of Solomon

Magic Ring of Solomon

Secret Seal of Solomon

Seals of Solomon - Lesser Keys of Solomon

SIGILLAGRAPHIA

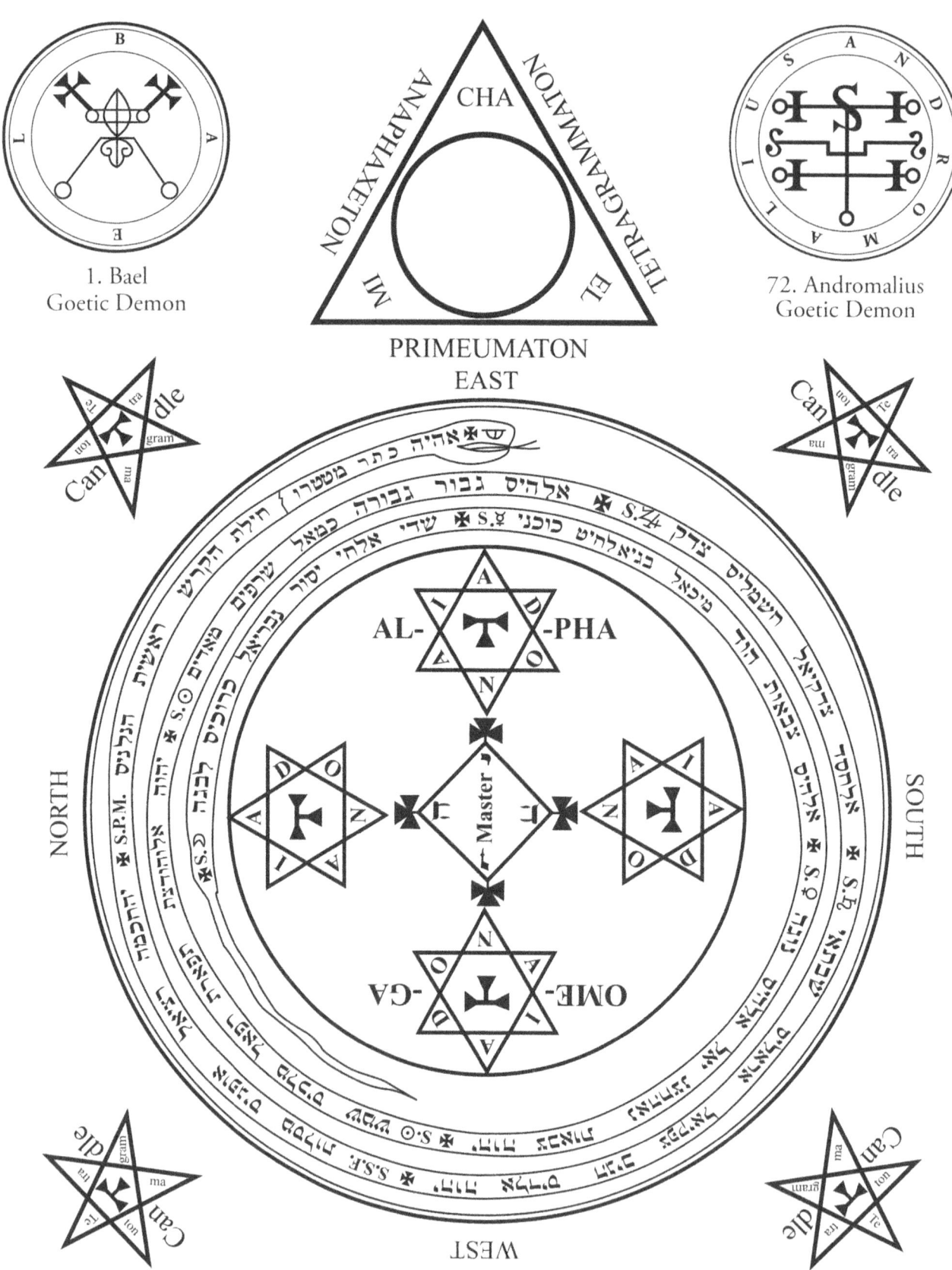

Circle of Evocation - Lesser Keys of Solomon (Golden Dawn 19th C.)

Table of Practise

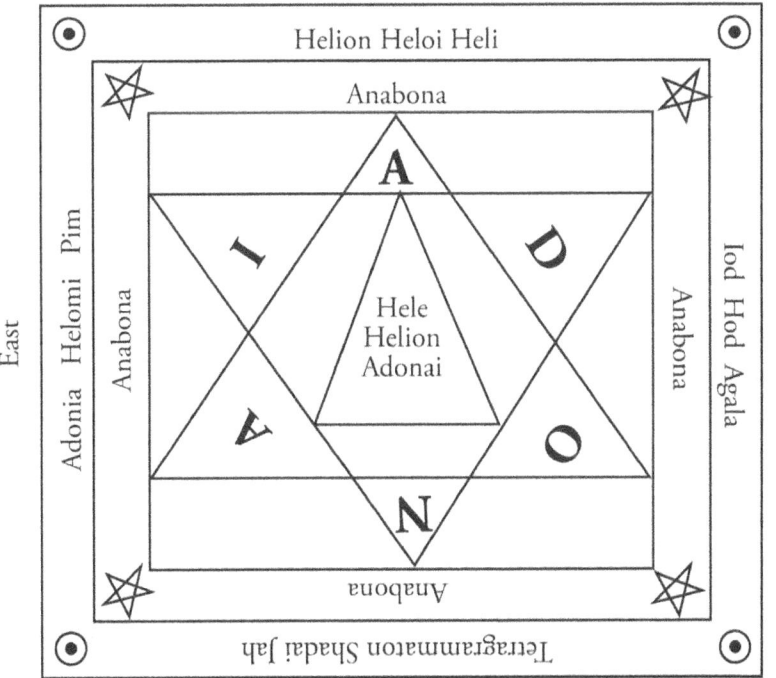

Almadel (Portable Alter)

Tables of Conjuration - Lesser Keys of Solomon

SIGILLAGRAPHIA

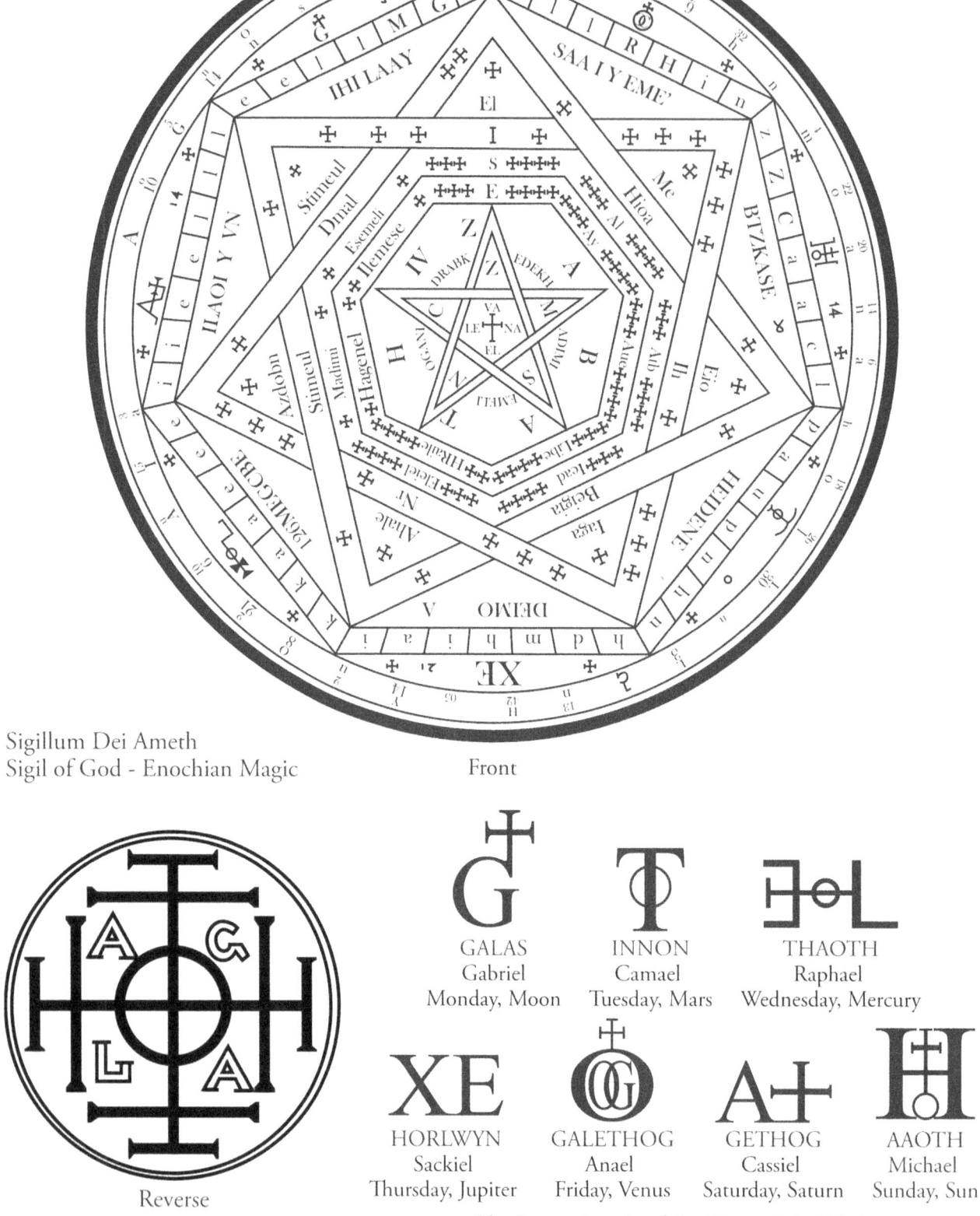

Sigillum Dei Ameth
Sigil of God - Enochian Magic

Front

Reverse

GALAS — Gabriel — Monday, Moon
INNON — Camael — Tuesday, Mars
THAOTH — Raphael — Wednesday, Mercury
HORLWYN — Sackiel — Thursday, Jupiter
GALETHOG — Anael — Friday, Venus
GETHOG — Cassiel — Saturday, Saturn
AAOTH — Michael — Sunday, Sun

The Seven Angels of the Days of the Week

RENAISSANCE

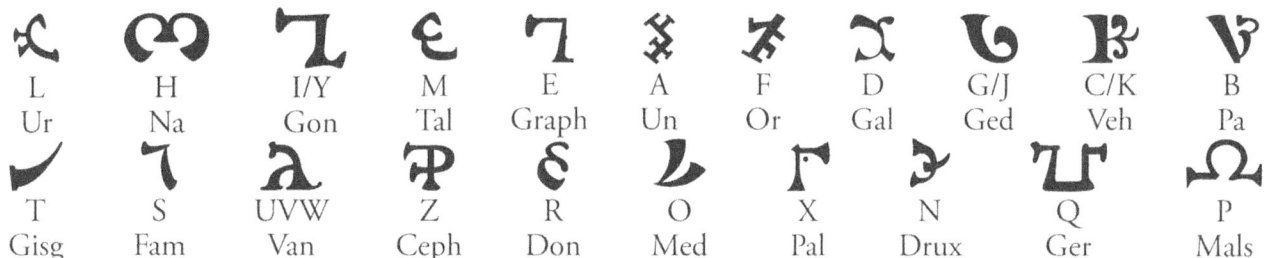

Dr John Dee's Angelic/Adamic/Enochian Alphabet (right to left) 1587

Great Table - Black Cross / Four Watchtowers (Four Elemental Spirits)
(Hermetic Order of the Golden Dawn)

Element - Water	Element - Air	Element - Earth	Element - Fire
Direction - West	Direction - East	Direction - North	Direction - South
Colour - Yellow	Colour - Blue	Colour - Black	Colour - Red
Spirit - TA HAO EL OG	Spirit - THA HE BY O A AT NUN	Spirit - THA HAA OTH E	Spirit - O HEOO AA A TAN

Seals of the Four Elementry Spirits and their Correspondences

SIGILLAGRAPHIA

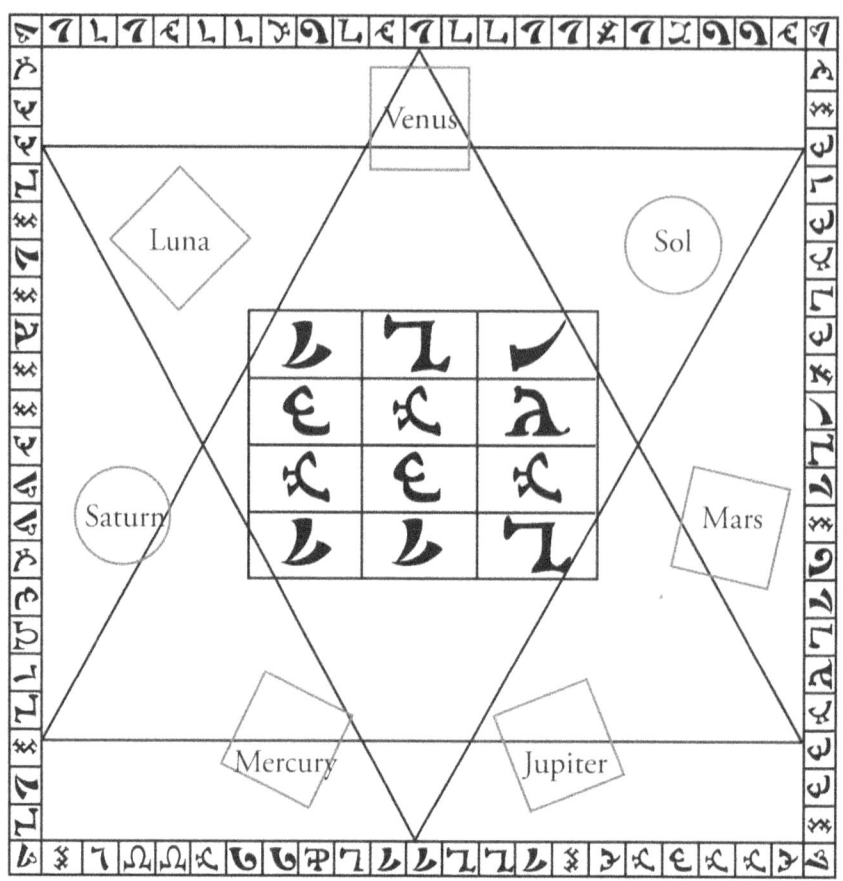

Holy Table of Practise

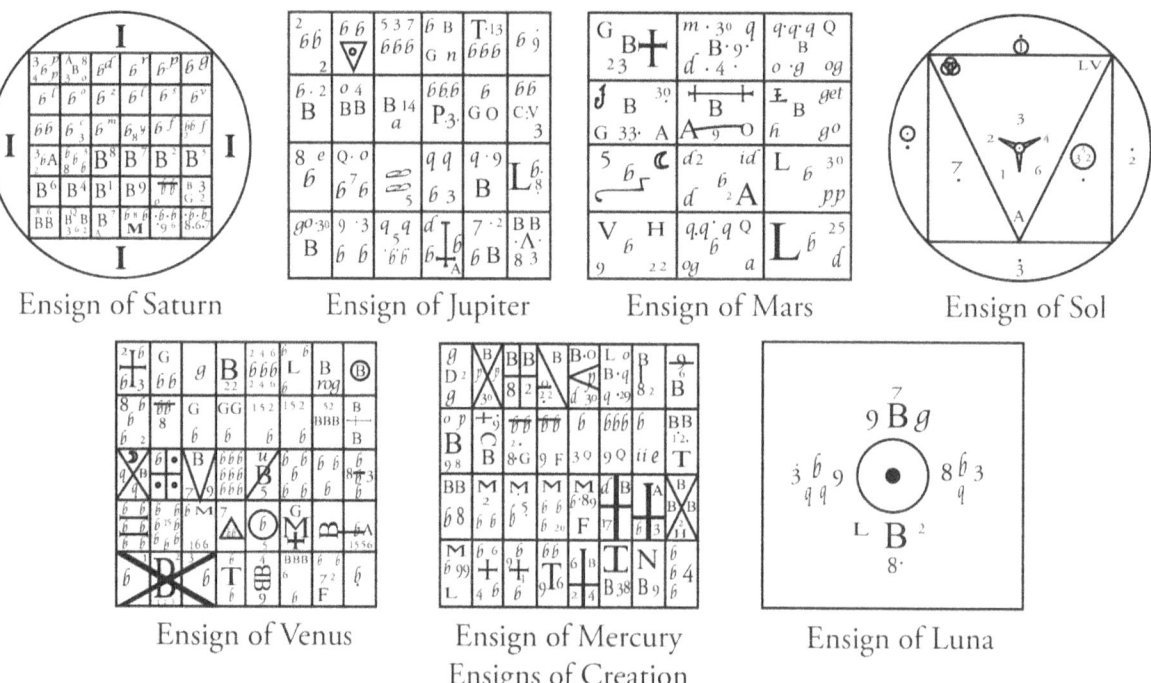

Holy Table of Practice and the Ensigns of Creation - Enochian Magic

Modern and Postmodern World
1600–2025

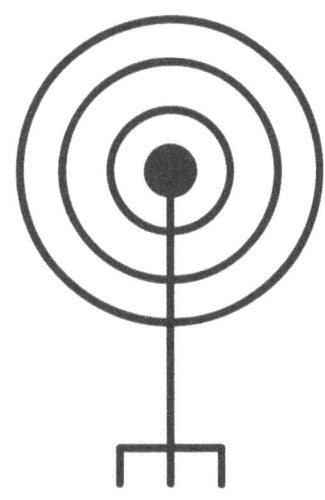

Modern World 1600–1945

The early modern world, 1600–1800, began with the Age of Science. At this time, the invention of the polished glass lens for telescopes and microscopes turned astrology into astronomy and alchemy into chemistry. Together with the Age of Enlightenment, starting in 1700, they introduced new concepts to European society and these ideas continue to permeate post-modern society.

As the influence of magic on the European intellect faded, the transmission of Western occult knowledge was continued by the Rosicrucians and Freemasons into the Late Modern period. Manuscripts on the conjuration of spirits continued to be published in the Modern Era, when they became known as grimoires, as in 'The Magus' by Francis Barrett in 1805. Other notable occultists of the time were Eliphas Levi and Albert Pike.

Following the invention of printing in 1445, published copies of magical texts were carried from mainland Europe to Scandinavia and the New World, influencing the design of the Icelandic rune staves called Galdrastafir and the Voodoo Veves of Haiti.

Now reclassified as Neopagan, Voodoo is a New World religion derived from the West African Voudoun tradition of Benin. Voodoo combines native African beliefs with European Catholicism, as slaves were not allowed to practice their own religion.

It is primarily practiced in the Caribbean, especially Haiti and New Orleans, where printed copies of the French 'Grand Grimoire' or 'Red Dragon' were taken in the 1800s and thought to have influenced the design of Voodoo Veves.

The Icelandic runes called Galdrastafir are a mixture of Viking and Christian magic created between 1400 and 1800. Their design is thought to be heavily influenced by the symbols found in fourteenth century Greek copies of Solomonic magic. With the rise of Neopaganism, they were revived by the Geatish Society in the nineteenth century. In the 1970s and 80s, they became recognized as symbols associated with the Icelandic Heathen religion of Asatru, or 'Native Faith'.

Neopaganism is an Earth-centered movement based around the revival of pre-Christian indigenous religions of Europe, North Africa and the Near East. The term is also applied to those native religions revived by the indigenous peoples of the Americas, Africa, Australia and Asia, a forced reaction to combat the cultural appropriation created by Christianization and New Age eclecticism. It is also applied to anti-Christian religions such as Satanism.

There are two main forms of Neopaganism. Reconstructionist movements, like Heathenism, romanticize the past. Eclectic movements, like Wicca and the New Age, idealize the future. Both aim to create a system in which humans can live in harmony with the Earth and its cycles.

'Heathen' is a Christian term used to describe the pre-Christian native religions of Europe. In the nineteenth century, it was only used to refer to those who prayed to a Norse/Germanic pantheon of gods. In more modern usage, it is a broad term referring to the polytheistic religions of Greece, Italy, Britain, Germany, Scandinavia, Eastern Europe, Baltic States, Ukraine, Russia and Armenia.

Prior to World War II, German and Polish groups were referred to as Neopagan. Today, most of these groups prefer the term Heathen. They consider themselves to be reconstructed religions—as close to the original as they can get—and as a part of a tradition separate from Neopaganism; not a branch of it, but a separate tree.

Heathenism does not have a unified ideology, preferring the term 'Native Faith' to describe its religion. Its pantheon centers on deities from pre-Christian Germanic Europe such as Tyr, Odin, Thor, Frigg and Freya from Scandinavia, while Woden and Eostre are Anglo-Saxon.

Heathen groups share the same Indo-European mythology and symbology as other Neopagan groups, having their own ethnic or regional systems in which rune magic plays a central role.

In the European pagan mystical tradition, runes were employed as a mystic symbol system before they were adapted into a writing system.

The runes were not invented – they were, and are, seen as pre-existing forces handed down from eternity. They are considered intrinsically magic by their very nature. They promote communication, not only between men, but between mankind and deities, allowing for a conversation with the hidden powers that animate the world.

Originally, pagans looked to marry Christian theology with the concept of 'Native Faith'. Today, more modern Heathen extremists and New Age acolytes use paganism as way of rejecting Judeo-Christianity which, as they see it, outlawed their native traditions and culture.

In the seventeenth century, the notion of paganism changed from a theological aspect to an ethnological one. At this time, people's approach to paganism ranged from presenting ancient Greek Hellenism as a viable alternative to Christianity, to those who took an interest in paganism from the point of view of the noble savage.

The origins of Neopaganism began with the eighteenth and nineteenth century intellectual reaction to the scientific rationale of the Age of Enlightenment, and the rejection of Renaissance Neoclassicism in favour of a glorified view of Medievalism by the Romanticists who portrayed historic Celtic, Slavic and Germanic polythesis as the 'Noble Savage'.

This, combined with a romanticized interest in European folklore, led to the emergence of Heathen groups such as the Viking movement in Scandinavia, the Volkish movement in Germany, and the rise of Druidism in Austria and Switzerland (home of the pre-Celtic Hallstatt culture).

At the end of the nineteenth century, Neopaganism came to the fore through various international events. The biggest among these was the discovery of Tutankhamun's tomb in the 1920s, which created a growing interest in Egyptology.

Paralleled by the rise of Spiritualism in the USA and the creation of New Age philosophies such as Theosophy and Thelema, eventually things cohered enough to become known as the Neopagan Movement (to distinguish it from classical paganism, lasting from 1870 to 1920).

By 1933, German Heathenism had degenerated into the racial, ethnic and cultural exclusivity of the Aryan occultism associated with the Nazi Party, although they outlawed secret societies with their anti-freemasonary act of 1935.

German Heathenism largely disappeared following WWII, only to reappear in the 1970s as disbanded groups reformed in West Germany. The 1980s and 90s saw the rise of neo-Nazi inspired Heathen groups in Europe, USA and Australia.

Following the collapse of Communism in Eastern Europe, many Slavic Neopagan and Heathen groups reformed, not only practising the Slavic Native Faith of 'Rodnovery', but also mixing it with Indo-European traditions from Hinduism and Zoroastrianism.

Neopaganism is also associated with the New Age. The main difference between the two is that the New Age focusses on an improved future, whereas Neopaganism focusses on the pre-Christian past.

What they do have in common is the revolutionary concept of the 'Age of Aquarius', which provides both movements with a millenarianistic metaphor that allows and encourages a framework for radical change in thought patterns and their means of implementation.

The New Age movements of the twentieth century have their roots in Theosophy, with its mainly Hindu and Buddhist concepts. Meaning 'Godly Wisdom', Theosophy originated with Russian-born occultist Madame Helena Blavatsky in the 1870s.

She borrowed many ideas from Hinduism, Buddhism and German mythology, believing that the Ascended Masters are attempting to revive knowledge of an ancient tradition—once found across the world—that will come again to eclipse all existing world religions.

Thelema is an esoteric and occult society of spiritual thought developed in the early 1900s by English magician Aleister Crowley. Just like the Theosophists, Crowley was inspired by Indian and Chinese philosophy, but is more associated with the Egyptian and Greek rites of the Hermetic Order of the Golden Dawn, amongst others.

To a certain degree, Crowley's thought in general inspired the rise of Neopaganism, and he became a significant influence upon the founders of new religious movements and occultists including Gerald Gardner, founder of Wicca; Ross Nichols, who developed Druidism; Austin Osman Spare, whose occult philosophies became a cornerstone of Chaos Magick; and Anton LaVey, founder of the Church of Satan.

SIGILLAGRAPHIA

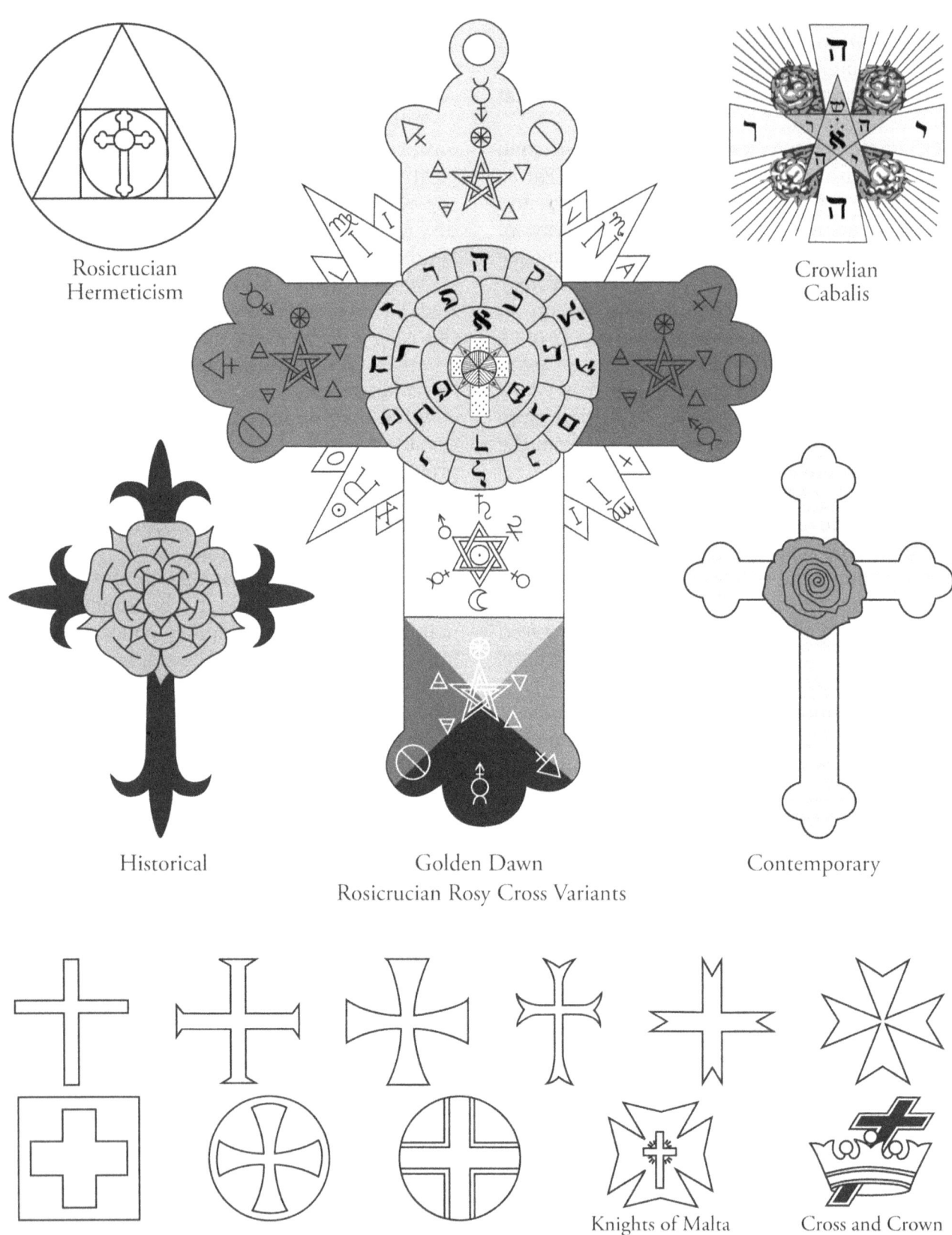

Rosicrucian Hermeticism

Crowlian Cabalis

Historical   Golden Dawn   Contemporary
Rosicrucian Rosy Cross Variants

Knights of Malta   Cross and Crown

Red Cross variants of the Knights Templar of St. John - Freemasonary

MODERN WORLD

Masonic Symbols

SIGILLAGRAPHIA

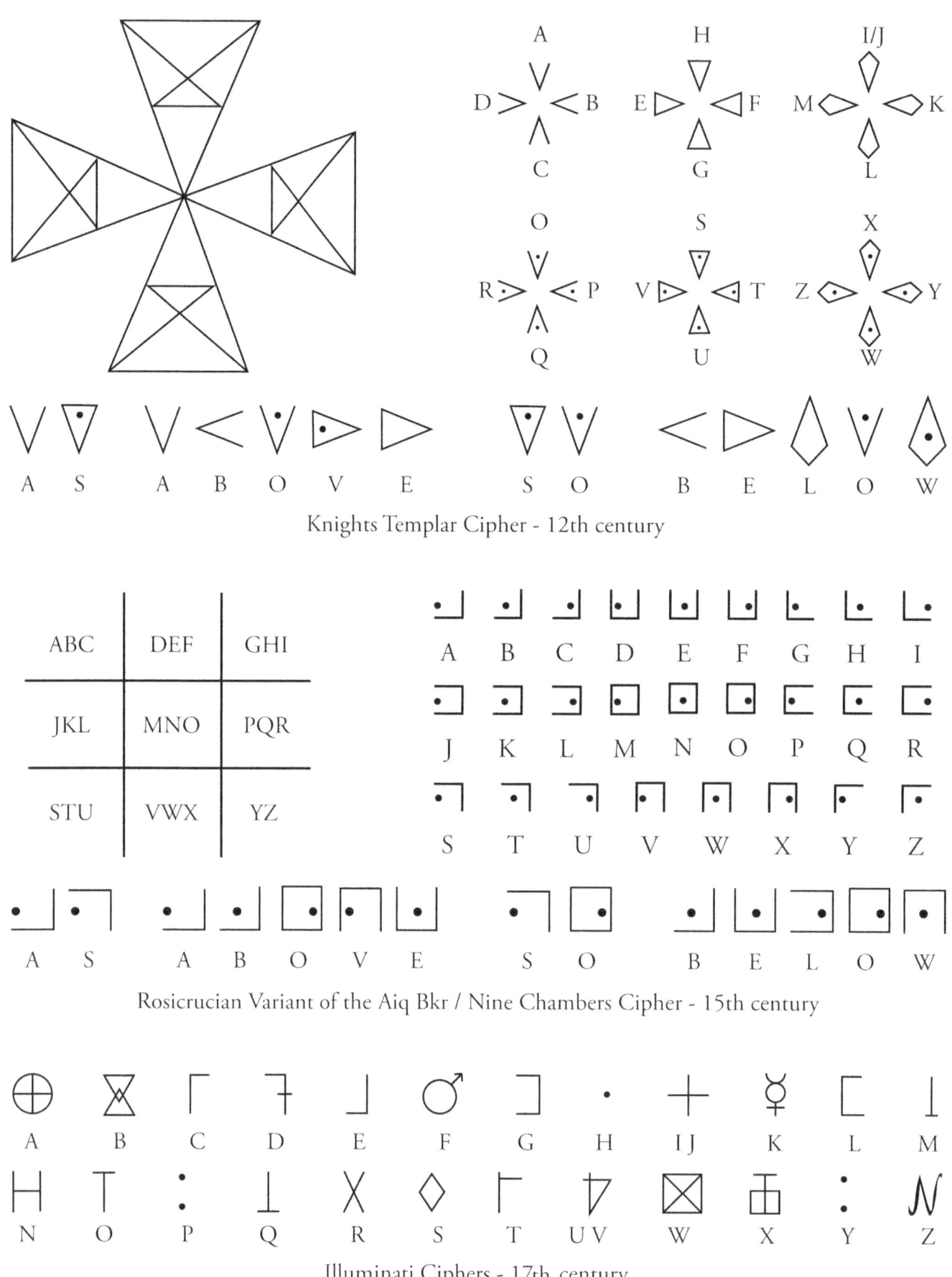

Knights Templar Cipher - 12th century

Rosicrucian Variant of the Aiq Bkr / Nine Chambers Cipher - 15th century

Illuminati Ciphers - 17th century

MODERN WORLD

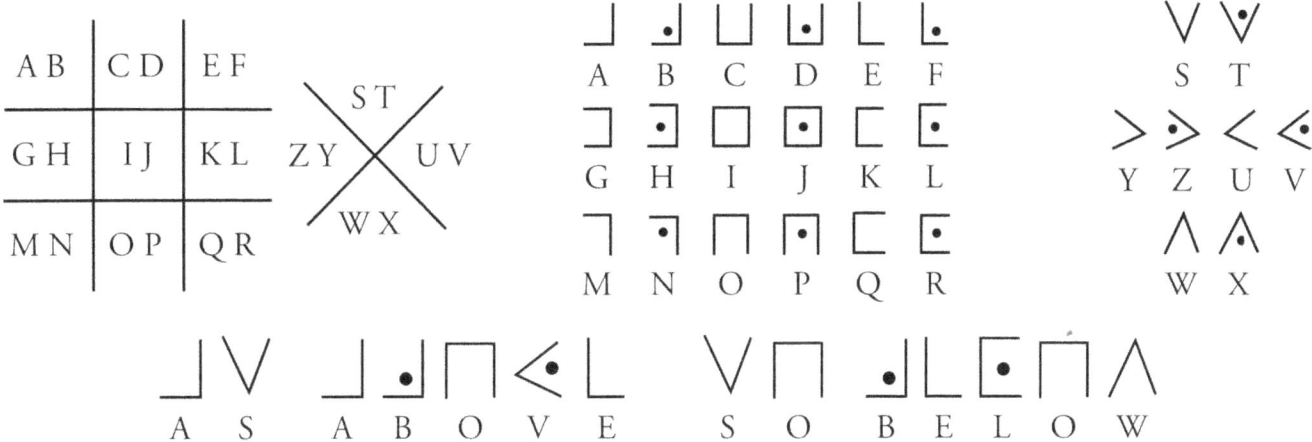

Royal Arch Cipher of the Freemasons

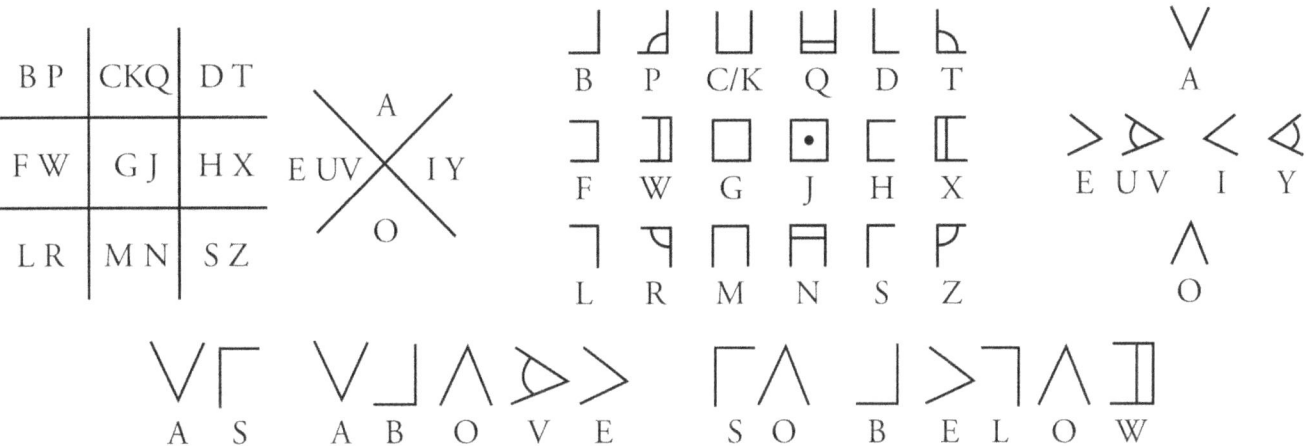

Nug Soth Variant of the Royal Arch Cipher

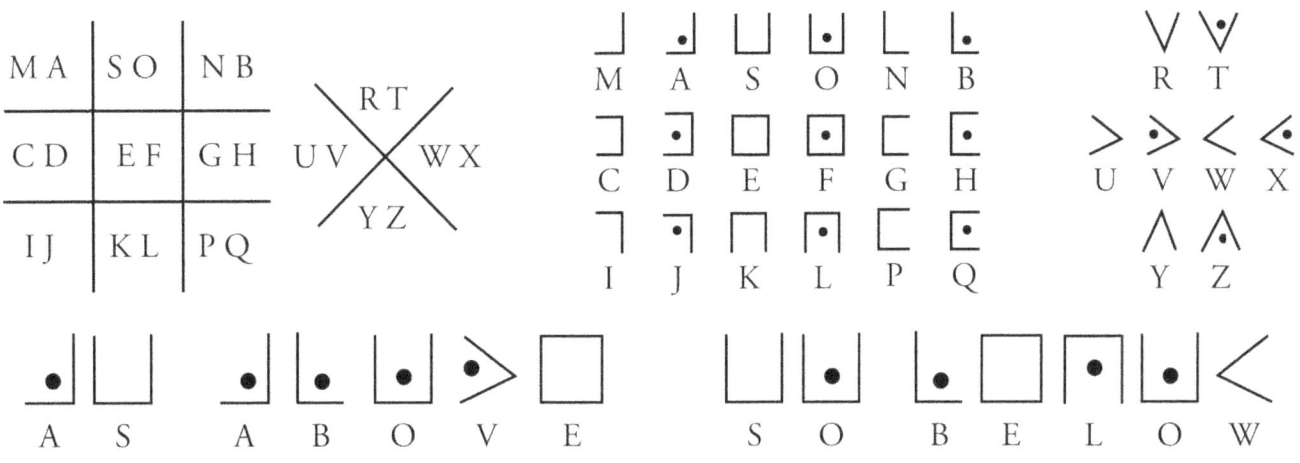

Blue Loge Cipher

Masonic 'Pig Pen' Ciphers

SIGILLAGRAPHIA

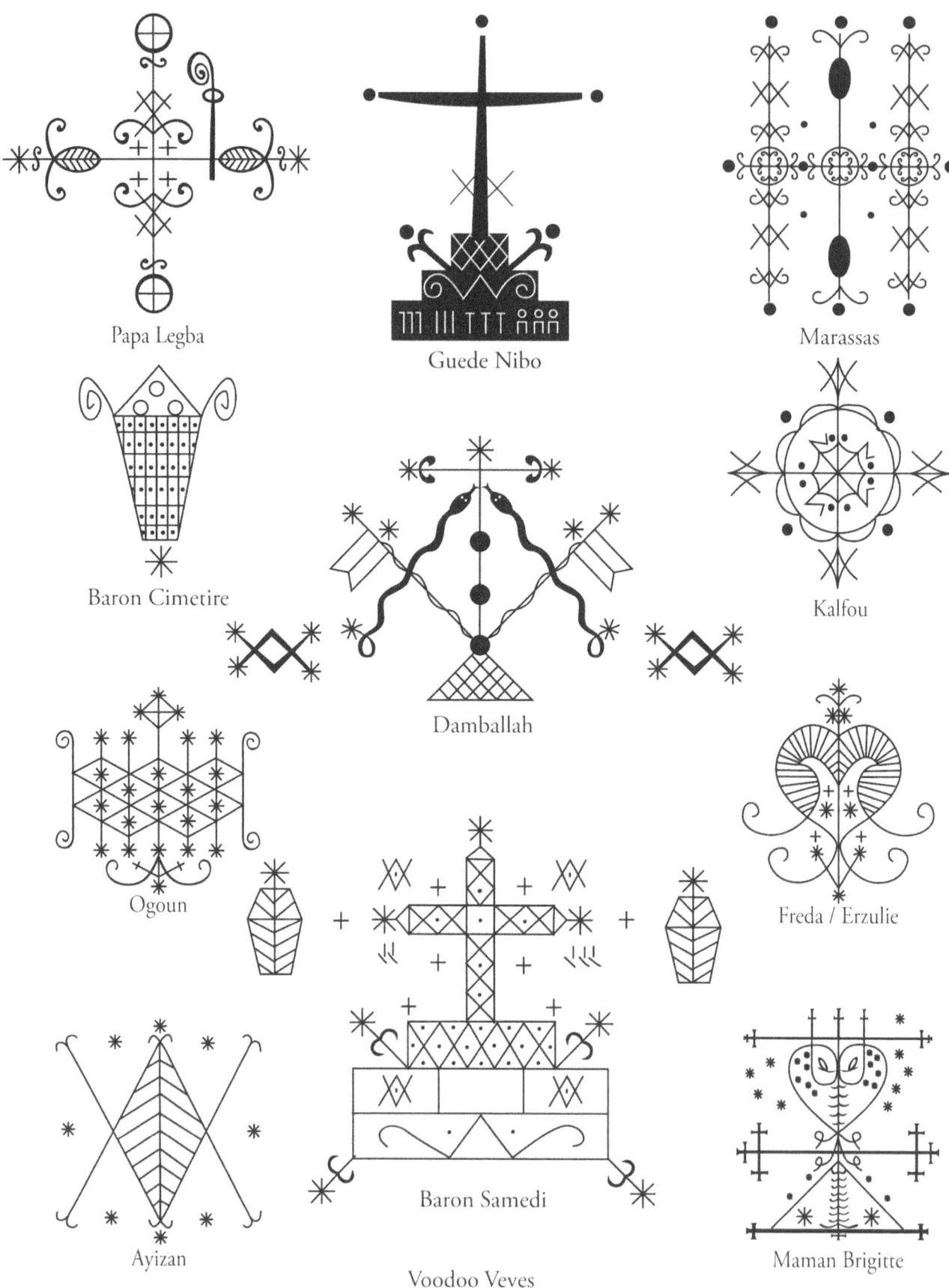

Voodoo Veves

MODERN WORLD

Galdrastafir - Icelandic Rune Staves

SIGILLAGRAPHIA

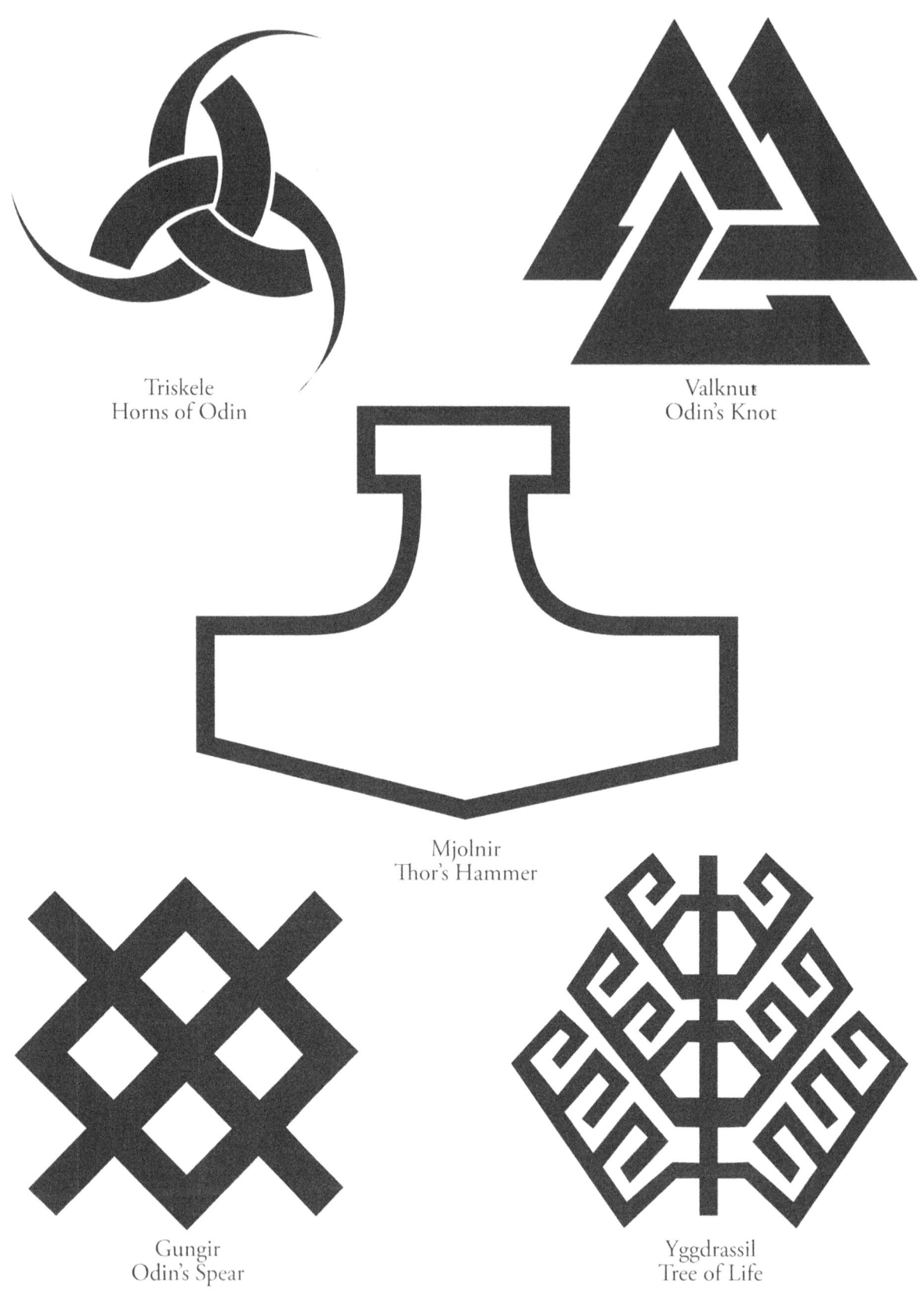

Triskele
Horns of Odin

Valknut
Odin's Knot

Mjolnir
Thor's Hammer

Gungir
Odin's Spear

Yggdrassil
Tree of Life

Revived Symbolism of Norse / Germanic Heathenry

MODERN WORLD

Thor's Hammer　　　Gammadion　　　Fylfot Rune　　　Swastika

Broken Solar Cross

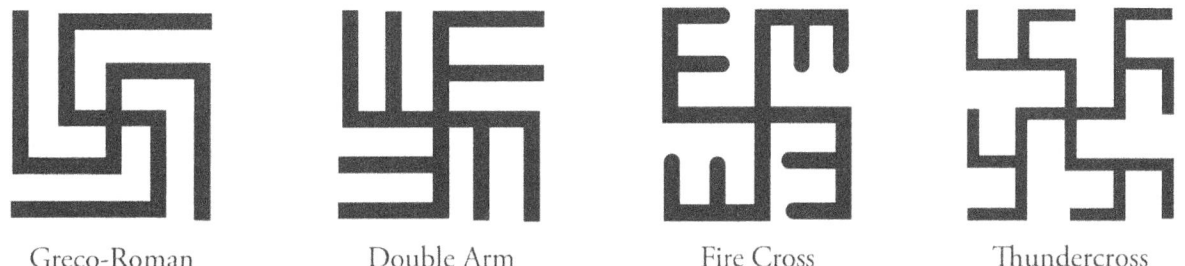

Greco-Roman　　　Double Arm　　　Fire Cross　　　Thundercross

Heathen Swastika Variants

SIGILLAGRAPHIA

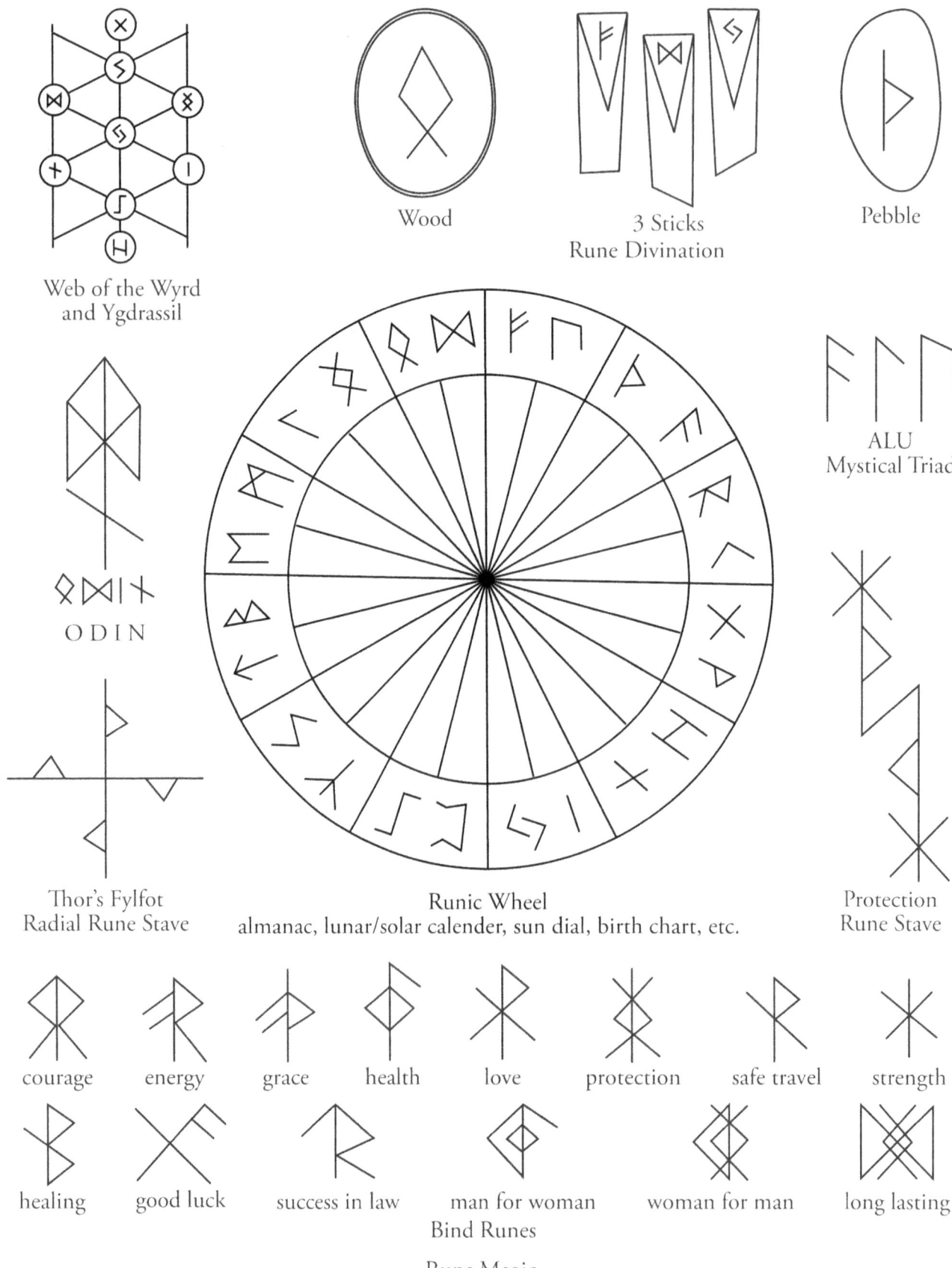

Web of the Wyrd and Ygdrassil

Wood

3 Sticks
Rune Divination

Pebble

ODIN

ALU
Mystical Triad

Thor's Fylfot
Radial Rune Stave

Runic Wheel
almanac, lunar/solar calender, sun dial, birth chart, etc.

Protection
Rune Stave

courage   energy   grace   health   love   protection   safe travel   strength

healing   good luck   success in law   man for woman   woman for man   long lasting

Bind Runes

Rune Magic

MODERN WORLD

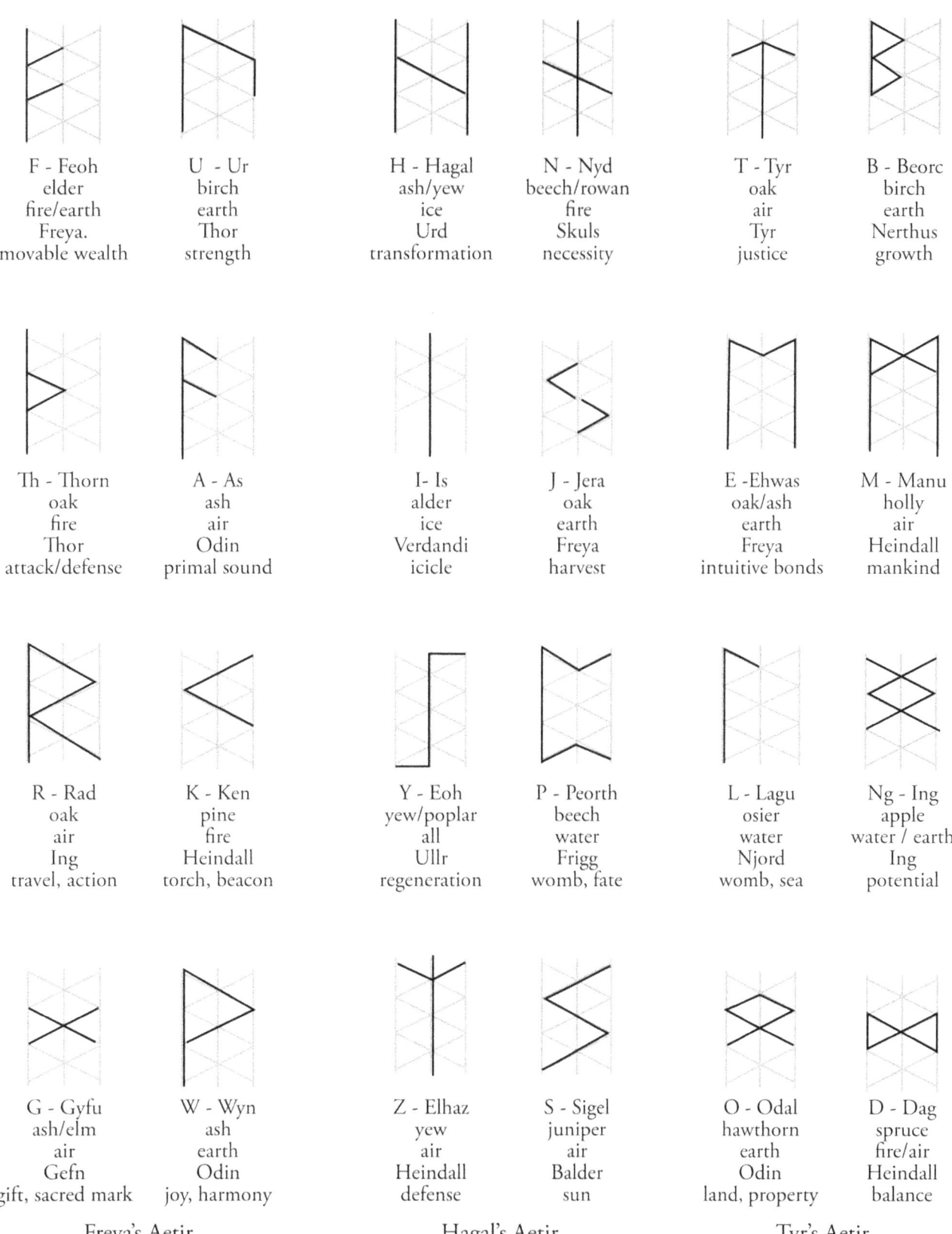

Runic Futhark, Aetir's and Correspondences

SIGILLAGRAPHIA

ᚠ	F - Fa - generate your luck and you will have it
ᚢ	U - Ur - know yourself, then you will know all
ᚦ	Th - Thurs - preserve your ego
ᚨ	A / O - Os - your spirit force makes you free
ᚱ	R - Rit - I am right, this rod right is indestructable, therefore, I am indestructable
ᚲ	K - Ka - your blood, your highest possession
ᚺ	H - Hag - harbour the All in yourself and you will control the All
ᚾ	N - Nor - use your fate, do not strive against it
ᛁ	I - Is - win power over youself and you will have power over everything in the spiritual and physical world
ᛅ	A - Ar - respect the primal fire
ᛋ	S - Sig - the creative spirit must conquer
ᛏ	T - Tyr - fear not death, it cannot kill you
ᛒ	B - Bar - the life strands in the hands of God, trust it in you
ᛚ	L - Laf - first learn to steer, then do the sea journey
ᛘ	M - Man - be a man
ᛦ	Y - Yr - think about the end
ᛂ	E - Em - marriage is the raw-root of the Aryan
ᚼ	G - Gibor - Man, be one with God

Armenan Runes (Aryan Cabala), Von List 1902

Adulrunen (Noble Runes) - Johnnes Bureus 1611

F	U	Th	A	R	K	H	N	I
1	3	5	7	9	10	30	50	70

E	S	T	B	L	M	Y
90	100	300	500	700	900	1000

Armanen Runes (Hitler Runes), Wiligut 1929

F, U, Th
O, R, K
H, N, I
Aah, S, T
B, L, M
Y, Eh, G

MODERN WORLD

Shutzstaffell / SS Runes - Nazi Runic Insignia, 1920-1945

SIGILLAGRAPHIA

Heathen Deity Symbols of the Slavic Native Faith 'Rodnov'

MODERN WORLD

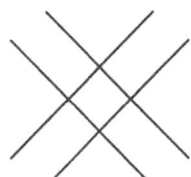

AKA
Double Cross
Sun & Energy
Unity & World Order
Water Well
Start of Agricultural Year

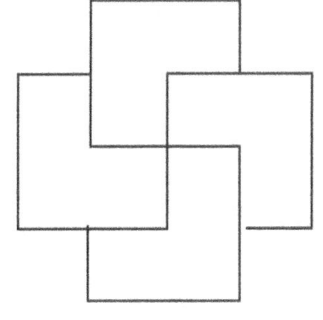

Tursaansydan
Finland

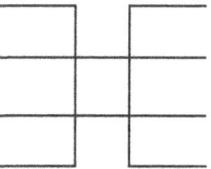

DZIVIBA
Light
New Beginnings
Life Journey
Strength
Protection

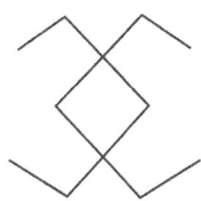

KRUPTIS
The Subconscious
Intuition
Knowledge
Wisdom
Strength

Svarga / God - Ynglist

AUSTRA'S TREE
World Order
Past, Present, Future
Beautiful & Valuable
Blessings
Success

ZALKTIS
Snake
The Changeable
Wisdom & Knowledge
Life Energy
Communication

Rantha - The Name of God
(Ynglist Runes)

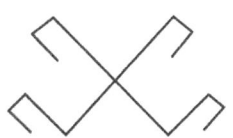

MARTINS
Embellishment of Jurnis
Productivity
Fertility
Prosperity

Finnish Runes and Russian Ynglism

SIGILLAGRAPHIA

Sanskrit Letter

Sacred Symbol
OM / AUM

Swastika

Theosophical Seal

Interlocking Hexagram

Ankh

Ouroubous

Theosophy / Madame Helena Blavatsky

MODERN WORLD

(Somaya) Mandala   Sri Yantra

Hinduism

Dharma Wheel   Lotus Flower   Tiratana

Buddhism

Taijitsu - Yin and Yang   Pakua / Bagau - Eight Trigrams   Enso

Daoism and Zen Buddhism

Symbols of Eastern Mysticism

SIGILLAGRAPHIA

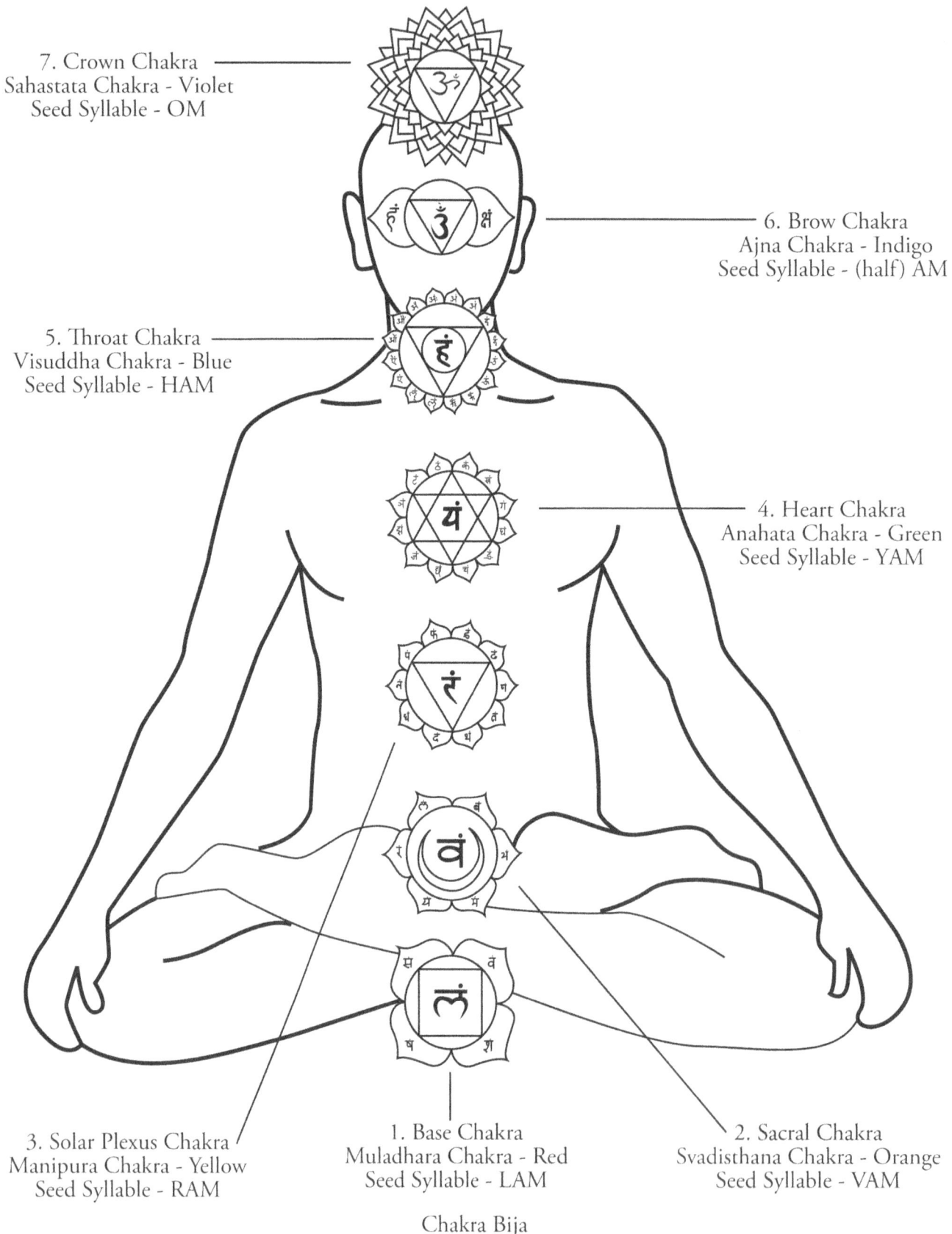

7. Crown Chakra
Sahastata Chakra - Violet
Seed Syllable - OM

6. Brow Chakra
Ajna Chakra - Indigo
Seed Syllable - (half) AM

5. Throat Chakra
Visuddha Chakra - Blue
Seed Syllable - HAM

4. Heart Chakra
Anahata Chakra - Green
Seed Syllable - YAM

3. Solar Plexus Chakra
Manipura Chakra - Yellow
Seed Syllable - RAM

1. Base Chakra
Muladhara Chakra - Red
Seed Syllable - LAM

2. Sacral Chakra
Svadisthana Chakra - Orange
Seed Syllable - VAM

Chakra Bija

MODERN WORLD

Astral drawings derived from Tantric aids to meditation and altered states of consciousness, using five elementary symbols to produce a set of 25 coloured symbols as an aid to visionary experiences. Hermetic Order of the Golden Dawn.

SIGILLAGRAPHIA

Wadjet / Eye of Horus

Hermetic Order of the Golden Dawn

Earth Pentacle

Hermetic Order of the Golden Dawn

Ordo Templis Orientalis

Unicursal Hexagram
Thelema

Lightening Bolt

Astrum Argentum

Cancellarius Seal

Mark of the Beast

Symbolism Associated with Aleister Crowley

78

MODERN WORLD

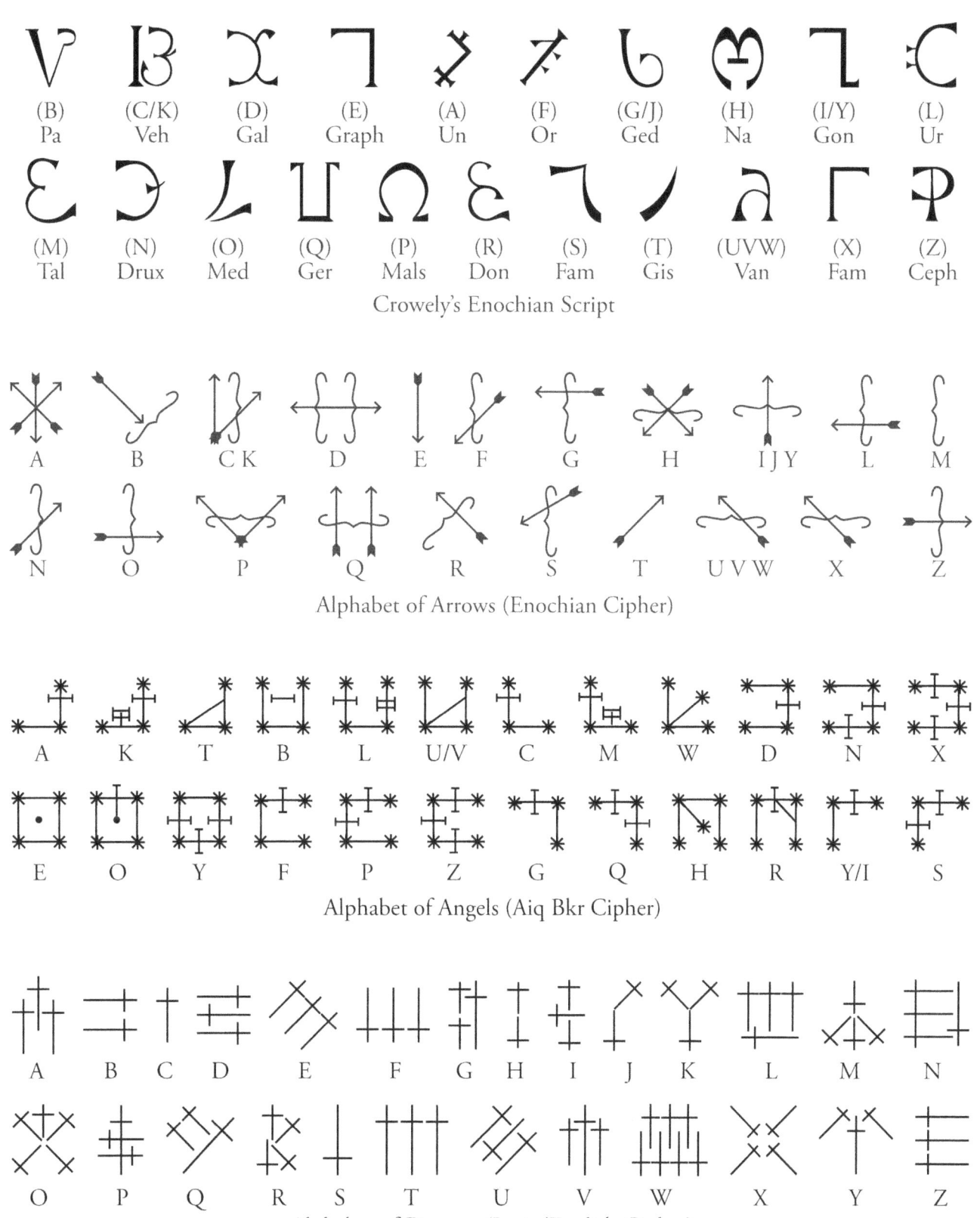

Aleister Crowley's Occult Scripts

SIGILLAGRAPHIA

Broken Solar Cross
Gemanic

Kolovrat / Swastika
Slavic

Goddess Chaxiraxi
Matriarcial Heathenism

Ankh
Kemeticism

Celtic

Hellenism

Traditional Roman Movement

Roma Nova

Arevakhach
Armenia

Romuva
Lithuania

Mordvin
Finland

Dievturita
Latvia

Baltic Cross

Runvira - Ukraine

Reconstructed Paganism - Heathenism / Native Faith

MODERN WORLD

Church of Aphrodite

Gender Diversity

Pagan Federation

Life and Earth
Core Shamanism

Extinction Rebellion
Eco-paganism

Eclectic Paganism - Witchcraft, Druidism, Earth, Goddess and Nature Worship

Mexicayotl
Native Aztec Religion

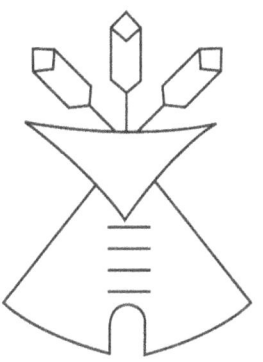

Native American Church
Peyote Religion

Red Road Church
Native / Christian Religion

Native American Movements

The Satanic Temple

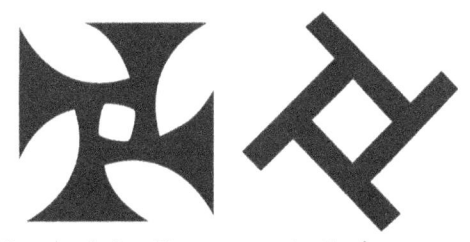

Original 60s Design   70s Redesign
Process Church of the Final Judgement
Satanic Churches

Septenary Sigil
Order of Nine Angels
Left-handed Satanists

Postmodern World 1945–2025

The postmodern world, much like the modern world, is defined by its advanced industrialism and materialism. It is also defined by its spiritual movements' rejection of it – Wicca, Druidry, Mother Earth, Nature and Goddess worship, Luciferianism and Satanism, Counter Culture, the New Age and Chaos Magick – all mainly British in origin.

As in Europe, British Neopaganism began with the Romantic movement of the eighteenth century and a renewed interest in ancient British and Celtic art, literature and religion. This inspired authors, artists, philosophers, scientists and lay people to increasingly turn to Celtic, Germanic, Egyptian, Greco-Roman, Eastern and other forms of paganism for inspiration.

Of the revived Indo-European symbols, Celtic knots appeared in the third and fourth centuries CE. They were derived from knot designs, like those used for the braiding and plaiting of hair, that were adapted into the ornamentation of Christian monuments and manuscripts such as the Book of Kells.

This revival continued throughout the nineteenth century as paganism came to the attention of British occultists through various international events and cultural developments, including fresh archeological discoveries in Egypt, a growing interest in ancient history and the formation of the Folklore Society in 1878. Aleister Crowley was a product of this.

By the early twentieth century, there were established Heathen brotherhoods, Druid groves and witches covens across Britain. After World War II, Neopagans began to re-establish Heathenism, Witchcraft and Druidry in Britain.

British Heathenism began with the first flourishing of Anglo-Saxon studies in the eighteenth and nineteenth centuries. Today, it is primarily present in two forms: Odinism, an international Heathen movement; and Anglo-Saxon Heathenism, called Esetroth or Fyrnsiou, meaning 'ancient custom' in Old English. Both forms draw from the Anglo-Saxon identity and culture of England, with almost no difference between them. The Odinic Rite was founded in England in 1973 and in 1988 became the first polytheistic religion to be awarded Registered Charity status.

There were two influential events – the first was in 1945, when Robert Graves published his book, 'The White Goddess', in which Celtic mythologies are reconstructed; the second was the repeal of the Witchcraft Act in 1951, which allowed Gerald Gardner to publish Witchcraft Today in 1954. These events not only gave rise to Wicca but to Neodruidism as well.

There are many similarities between Wicca and Neodruidism. Both emphasize the importance of developing a close link with nature. Both stress the importance of guardianship of the Earth and environmentalism.

Modern British Druidism has its roots in the Celtic revival of eighteenth century. Its first organized group was the Ancient Order of Druids and included the artist and Arch Druid William Blake. Founded in London in 1781 along Masonic lines, it is not considered Neopagan.

It was followed in 1792 by the Gorsedd of the Bards of the Isle of Britain. Its rituals form an important part of the Welsh National Eisteddfod. Its members include British royalty and senior clergy and it is not considered to be a Neopagan institution.

At the beginning of the twentieth century, George Watson MacGregor Reid began promoting Druidism as a spiritual path that could unite followers of many different faiths. This church, called the Universal Bond, became a vehicle for conveying the ideas of the Theosophical Society and the Golden Dawn.

In the 1940s and 50s, the Universal Bond evolved into the Ancient Druid Order, becoming the first such organization to be considered Neopagan. It attracted the catalytic figures of Ross Nichols and Gerald Gardner. Nichols developed Druidism, focusing on Celtic lore and mythology. Gardner become a seminal figure in Wicca. Both men were influenced by Aleister Crowley and Robert Graves' book, 'The White Goddess'.

In Celtic mysticism, Tree Ogham employs the initial letter of the names of trees arranged in sequential order for calendar-making.

This practice was common in the Bronze

Age, employed from Palestine to Ireland and universally associated with the Triple Moon Goddess of the three-season lunar year, before it was adapted to act as the four-season solar calendar of the Sun God.

The origin of this botanical system has its roots in the seasonal plants, shrubs and trees found in the Rhinelands of Switzerland and Austria, home of the ancestral Iron Age Celtic 'La Terne' culture.

The Celts believed that humans were descended from trees. Because of this, trees played an important role in their religious beliefs.

Celtic Druids were said to be able to manipulate the alphabet to create sounds that brought about creation or manifestation. These sounds were correlated by bards—druids who specialized in music—to correspond to musical notes, which were said to incite inanimate objects at the Druid's will.

The tally arrays of Ogham script form individual letters called 'fews'. In the Tree Ogham alphabet there are 20 fews and these are set out into four sets of five (called 'groves') to represent the seasons. The fews represent the months, and the groves represent the equinoxes and solstices of the lunar and solar calendars.

Post-war paganism remained underground until the emergence of 1960s Counter Culture. By 1969, Druids were starting to appear in the Counter Culture thanks to John Lennon's realization that Peace and Love, as the cornerstone of Counter Culture revolution, connected with Druidism. More overtly, Neodruid groups developed in Britain from the 1970s onwards, including the British Druid Order and the Druid Network.

During the Counter Culture there was a growth in shamanism and witchcraft that was noticeably influenced by feminism, leading to Earth, Nature, Mother and goddess worship. This was paralleled by the rise of Luciferian and satanic cults in the late 60s and early 70s.

The 1980s were dominated by the boom in New Age movements, when Wicca and goddess cults—influenced by feminism—produced Dianic Wicca. In the same decade, Faery Wicca and LGBT gender rights groups emerged from eclectic paganism, as did the eco-paganism of the early twenty-first century, which has its roots in Wicca – the largest of all the British Neopagan religions (with Druidry second).

British Neopagan scripts fall into two categories: those that have been revived from the past; and those new scripts based on pagan symbolism with no occult or literary history. Of all the British Neopagan scripts, the most authentic are the Barddas, or Bardic, runes. These runes were used to write the Welsh Druidic text called The Barddas. The Biobel Loath script was revived by the nineteenth century Celtic Romantics. 'Pecti Wita' is the modern revival name for Scottish or ancient Pictish paganism. The script has no antiquity and is used mainly for fortune-telling.

Traditional British witchcraft is a non-Wiccan (or pre-modern) form of the craft, especially if it has been inspired by historical forms of witchcraft and folk magic. Forms of traditional witchcraft include the Feri tradition, Cochrane's Craft and the Sabbatic Cult.

Developed in the first half of the twentieth century, Wicca or Wycca (Wittja) is an old Anglo-Saxon word meaning witch. Its Americanization by the popular media has adapted the word to include natural magic, or white witchcraft.

Wicca is generally a duotheistic religion, worshipping the Triple Moon Goddess and Horned God. Wiccans practice witchcraft and nature worship and claim its origins lie in pre-Christian Celtic religion, but most Wiccans draw their inspiration from the Book of Shadows – a book of rituals and spells compiled by Gerald Gardner, who is regarded as the father of modern witchcraft.

Named after Diana—the Roman equivalent of the Greek Goddess Artemis—Dianic Wicca is an eclectic form of British traditional witchcraft, European folk magic and healing practices from various other cultures and feminism. It is not a part of the Wiccan religion.

The primary text of Dianic Wicca is the 'The Holy Book of Women's Mysteries', written by its founder Zsuzsanna Budapest, who self-identifies as an 'hereditary witch', claiming to have learnt magic from her mother.

According to academics, the New Age has existed in many forms since the second century CE. Beginning with Gnosticism, New Age ideas have continued through a variety of groups including the Rosicrucians, Freemasons and Theosophists. The New Age movements of the late twentieth century have their roots in Theosophy, with its chiefly Hindu-Buddhist religious concepts.

The early New Age movement was based largely in Britain and is most associated with the Counter Culture of the 1960s. Some academics say that the direct descendents of the New Age can be found in the UFO religions of the 1950s.

The Dearinth is the logo of the Church of All Worlds, designed and co-founded in 1962 by the American wizard Oberon Zell. The symbol represents a labyrinth that includes the figures of the God and Goddess. The nine concentric circles represent the nine levels of initiation within the Church. Zell was the first to apply the term 'Neopagan' to the newly emerging Nature religions of the 1960s, and was instrumental in the coalescence of the movement in the 1970s.

At the end of the 1960s, many former members of the Counter Culture became early adherents of the New Age movement that emerged throughout the 70s and entered its full development in the early 80s, influencing British rave culture in the 90s. As an eclectic movement, the New Age mixes Eastern mysticism, UFO religion, shamanism and Neopaganism with alternative lifestyles, politics and pop culture.

The Goddess movement began in the nineteenth century, when first-wave feminists published their ideas on the female deity. At the same time, anthropologists examined the idea of prehistoric matriarchal culture. It is said that these theologies were suppressed when Christianity outlawed all concepts of there being an ancient religion.

These ideas gained greater influence during the second wave of feminism in the 1960s and 70s. Since then, Goddess worship has emerged as a recognizable international cultural movement.

Divine Feminine energy is simply the physical manifestation of all creative energy – the 'true' survival energy. The Spiral Goddess represents internal feminine power. The spiral represents the creative power within that corresponds to the sacred chakra of menstruation, our desires, our sexuality and our relationships.

The tradition of the Primordial Goddess can be seen reflected in many different conceptions of the Divine Feminine, including the Great Goddess, the Mother Earth Goddess, the Triple Goddess and the Goddess as the Tree of Life.

Goddess religions, especially those that worship a single Great or Mother Goddess, emphasize the relationship between femininity and nature. Many people involved in the Goddess movement regard the Earth as a living goddess. Gaia, or Gaea, was the Greek Goddess of the Earth – one of the primordial elemental deities born at the Dawn of Creation.

Earth-centered or Nature worship is a religious system based on the veneration of natural phenomena. It only covers religions that worship the Earth, Nature or a fertility deity, such as the various forms of goddess worship or matriarchal religions. It first came to the fore in the modern world as part of the New Age movement that grew out of the Counter Culture.

From the 1970s onward, those involved in the New Age were inspired to create modern magico-religious practices influenced by their idea of indigenous religions from across the world, creating what has been termed Neoshamanism.

Neoshamanism draws heavily from traditional shamanism. In Europe, it is from the nomadic traditions of Siberia and the Sami (Laplanders) of the Arctic Circle. In the Americas, it is those of Amazonian, Mesoamerican and Native American traditions.

Neoshamanism, or Western shamanism, seeks to reclaim what it sees as a lost heritage. It became a central theme of the New Age movement in the 1980s and 90s. Since then, the movement has been criticized by indigenous communities and the Christian Church for its 'misappropriation' of spiritual symbols and its practitioners ('plastic medicine people').

By the end of the 1960s, the positive white magic of the Age of Aquarius had been replaced by something darker – beginning with the Luciferian and Satanistic movements that emerged out of the Counter Culture, with roots in the antithesis or anti-hero of the Christian God.

Luciferianism began in the thirteenth or fourteenth century. It is attributed to a woman called Lucardis, who wanted to restore Lucifer to his righteous place in Heaven. This tradition remained unacknowledged until a resurgence in the nineteenth century.

Satanism is a modern construct based on his anti-Christ mythos and personalities. Crowley and Sloane developed its philosophies, inspiring Anton LaVey to compile the Satanic Bible and set up the Church of Satan in the 1960s.

Both Lucifer and Satan are represented using the same alchemical glyphs for sulphur, which is associated with the fire and brimstone of hell. Only Lucifer is associated with the light of phosphorous.

The late 1970s saw the publication of various editions of The Necronomicon – fake grimoires of demonic magic based on a fake grimoire created by horror writer H. P. Lovecraft in the 1920s. In a similar manner to that of the Keys of Solomon, it is now a recognized form of ceremonial magic.

Initially developed in England by Peter J. Carroll during the 1970s and 80s, Chaos Magick is a contemporary magical practice that draws heavily from the occult philosophies of English artist and mystic Austin Osman Spare.

At the beginning of the twentieth century, Aleister Crowley and Spare sought to reform aspects of ceremonial magic. Spare did this by refining the use of sigils by themselves, i.e. outside of ritual.

His 'sigilization' method dispensed with pre-existing esoterica and external beliefs. Sigils were no longer for controlling traditional demons and angels, but controlling forces in the unconscious psyche of the individual magician.

After his death, Spare's spiritual legacy was largely maintained by his friend, the Thelemite author Kenneth Grant, who studied with Crowley and Spare. He coined the term Zos Kia Cultus to refer to Spare's system of magic that involves complex symbolism deriving from sexual energy.

Grant helped to institute Spare's 'sigilization' as a cornerstone of Chaos Magick, since when it has become a popular practice among early twenty-first century Western occultists.

Chaos magicians have expanded on the basic sigilization technique, inventing new uses for sigils outside of ceremony. Gordon White developed the technique of 'shoaling', which involves launching a group of sigils for a set of related aims; instead of sigilizing for 'money', create a set of sigils for a pay rise, new business clients, a promotion or a chance win, etc – all of which help 'shift' the probability towards the overall aim.

The term 'hypersigil' was coined by Grant Morrison, who used it to refer to work of art that obtains magical meaning and willpower by becoming an extended artistic activity – taking the form of a poem, story, song or dance.

Chaos Magick also draws inspiration from pop culture. The Chaos Star symbol is a servitor constructed from eight arrow-headed spokes, representing the notion of infinite possibilities. It originated in the literary work of science-fantasy author Michael Moorcock's 'The Eternal Champions', published in the 1960s.

Created by the DKMU, the LS or linking sigil is an even more recent innovation, used to transfer energy from one place to another. The ELLIS linking sigil is the most famous variant.

In the early twenty-first century, Chaos Magick has been praised for breathing new life into Western occultism, but is criticized for a lack of initiatory knowledge. As a quick web search for magic sigils will reveal, a distinct amount of personal artistic styles have been created by amateur and serious sigilists alike.

A recent innovation in sigil design is the use of DTP software, where the sigil can be created using digital type, or even graphic fonts like MT Extra, as a cipher for English.

In 2007, Australian artist and occultist Barry William Hale published a grimoire of demonic magic titled 'Legion 49', in which he mixes Western high magic with the folk magic of old Mexico and the Haitian tradition.

His creative innovations include replacing the usual sigil used to conjure a spirit with an iconographical and sigillic recension of the Horde of 49 Servitors of Beelzebub, inspired by the protective symmetry of the paper cut tradition of old Mexico, called 'Papal Picardo' – a folk craft associated with the Day of the Dead alters.

To evoke these spirits, Hale created a Circle of Evocation—featuring the sigil of Beelzebub inside the Triangle of Arte, surrounded by some of the sigils of his 49 servitors—using Spare's 'sigilization' technique, thereby taking the sigil style back into ceremonial magic.

SIGILLAGRAPHIA

Trieskilon

Witch's

Solomon's

Shield

Triquetra

Shield

Celtic

Cross

Dara

Sailor's

Endless

Celtic Knots

POSTMODERN WORLD

Ancient Order of Druids

Awen
Order of Bards,
Ovates and Druids
Lollo Morganwg

Community Sigil
Anglo-Saxon Temple
Yeavering

Earth Mother
Reform Druids of
North America

Sigil of the Cosmos
American Druid Federation

The Druid Order

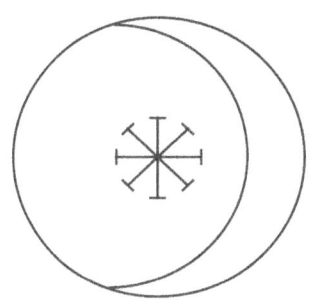

Seax Wicca
(Anglo-Saxon)

Community Sigil
Sporane Pagan
Village Community

Odinic Rite

Neopaganism Cult Symbols

SIGILLAGRAPHIA

Letter	Ogham	Irish	English	Date
B		Beth	Birch	Dec 25
L		Luis	Rowan	Jan 21
N		Nion	Ash	Feb 18
F(V)		Fearn	Alder	Mar 18
S		Saile	Willow	Apr 15

Consonants - Spring

Letter	Ogham	Irish	English	Date
H		Uath	Whitethorn	May 12
D		Duir	Oak	Jun 10
T		Tinne	Holly	Jul 8
C		Coll	Hazel	Aug 5
Q		Quert	Apple	Aug 5

Consonants - Summer

Letter	Ogham	Irish	English	Date
M		Muin	Vine	Sept 2
G		Gort	Ivy	Sep 30
Ng/Gn/P		Ngetal/Peth	Reed	Oct 28
Z/FF(F)		Straif	Blackthorn	Apr 15
R		Ruis	Elder	Nov 25

Consonants - Autumn

Letter	Ogham	Irish	English	Date
AA		Palm	Palm	NY Day
A		Alim	Silver Fir	New Year
O		Onn	Gorse/Furze	Spr. eqx
U		Ura	Heather	Sum. sols
E		Eadha	White Poplar	Aut. eqx
I		Idhu	Yew	Win. sols
II, J, Y			Mistletoe	Dec 23

Vowels - Winter

Ogham Staves

Tree Ogham Alphabet (BLN Variant) - Robert Graves / The White Goddess

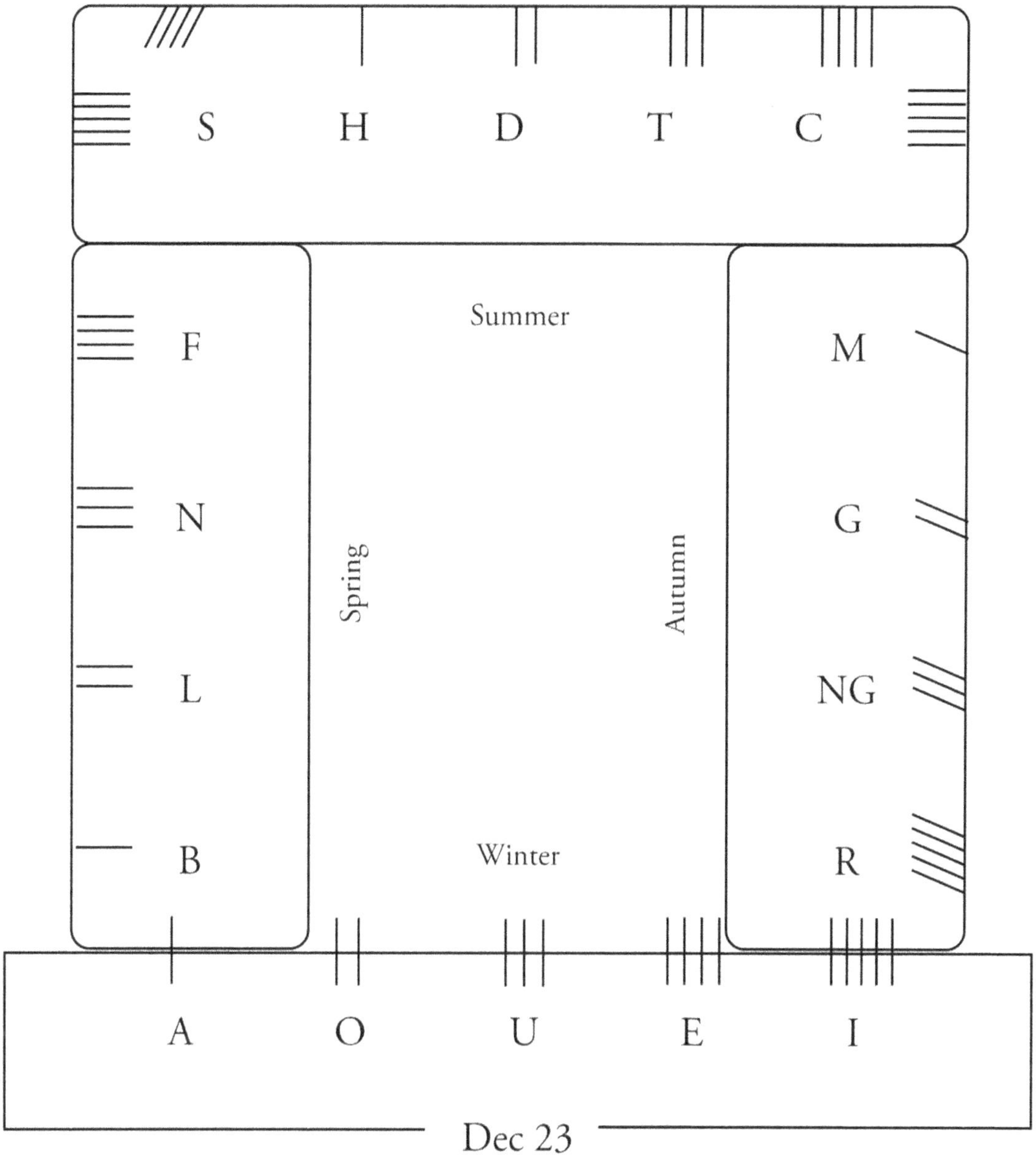

Stonehenge Lunar Calender Arrangement - Robert Graves / The White Goddess

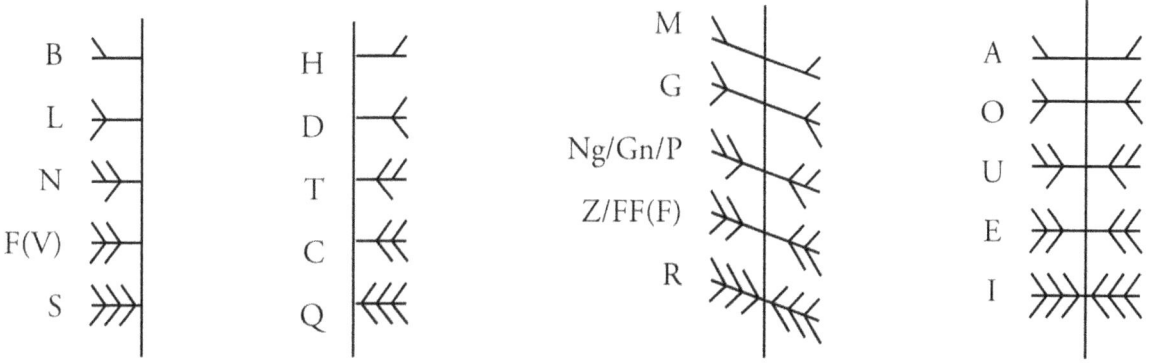

Branching Ogham Fews and Groves

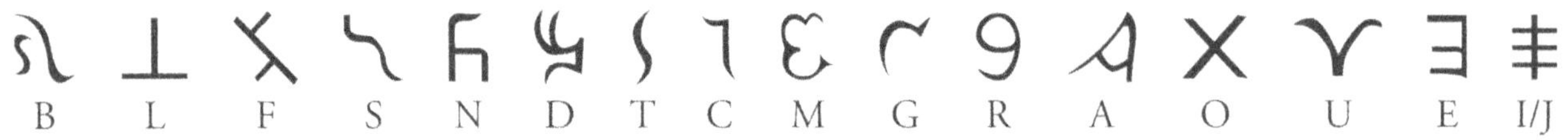

B L F S N D T C M G R A O U E I/J

Biobel Loath - Historical (Irish)

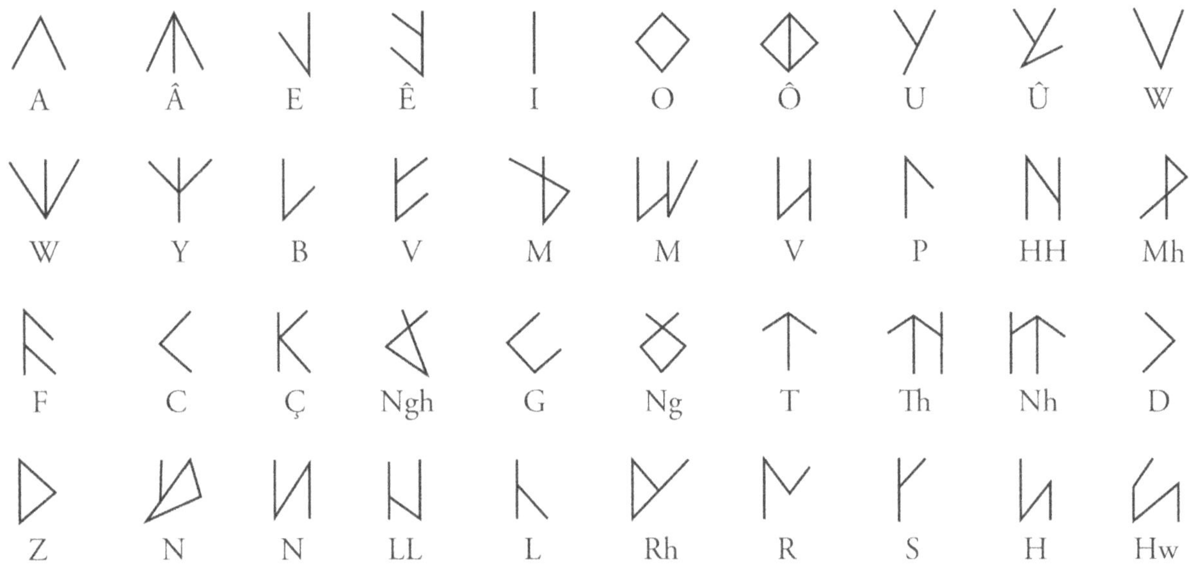

A Â E Ê I O Ô U Û W
W Y B V M M V P HH Mh
F C Ç Ngh G Ng T Th Nh D
Z N N LL L Rh R S H Hw

Bardas / Bardic Runes - Historical (Welsh)

A B C D E F G H I J K L M
N O P Q R S T U V W Y Z

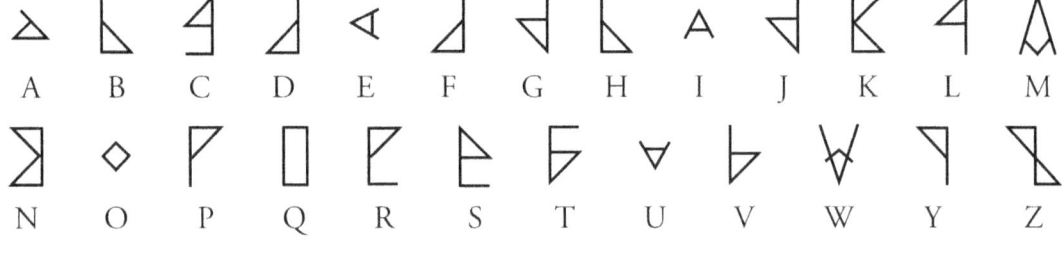

Pecti Wita Runes - Post Modern (Scottish)

A B C D E F G H I J K L M
N O P Q R S T U V W X Y Z

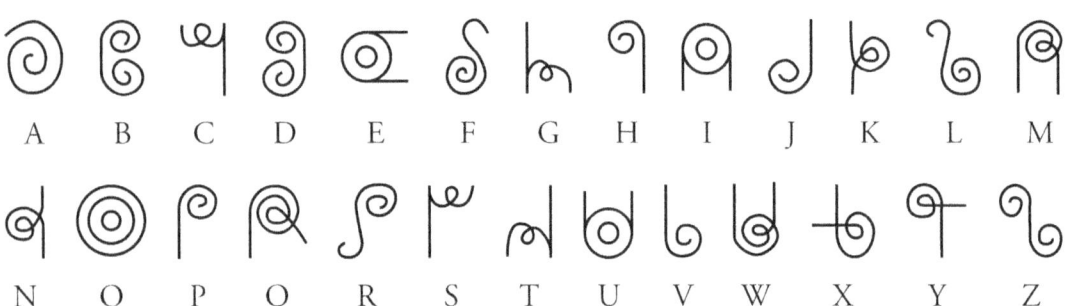

Pictish Swirls - Post Modern (Scottish)

Neopagan Scripts

POSTMODERN WORLD

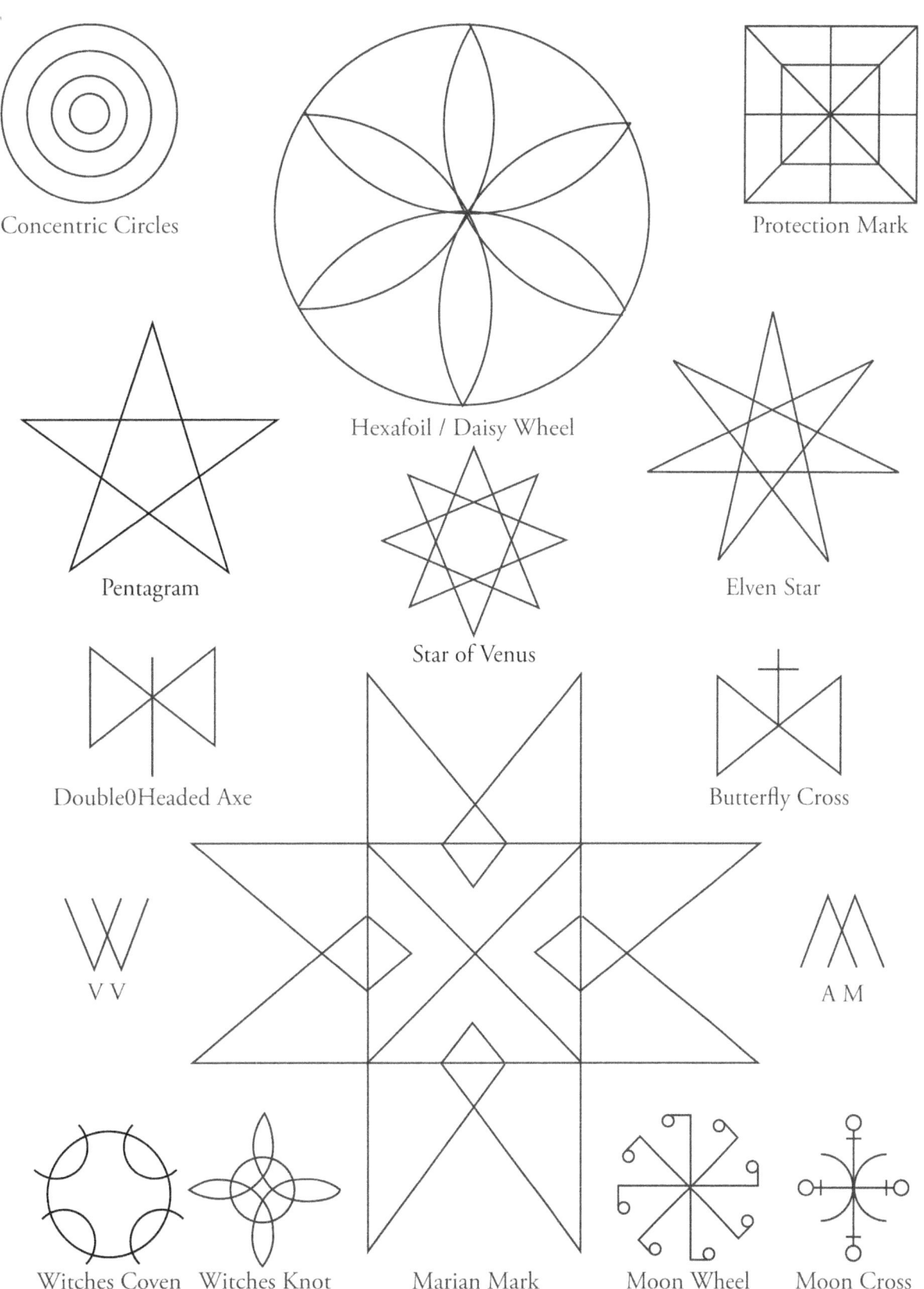

Concentric Circles

Protection Mark

Hexafoil / Daisy Wheel

Pentagram

Star of Venus

Elven Star

Double0Headed Axe

Butterfly Cross

V V

A M

Witches Coven

Witches Knot

Marian Mark

Moon Wheel

Moon Cross

Traditional Witchcraft Marks

SIGILLAGRAPHIA

Wiccan Pentagram / Female

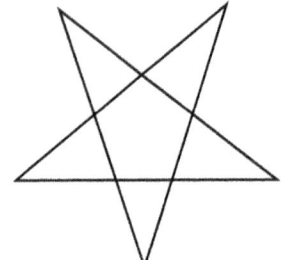
Satanic Pentagram / Male

Decagram - Union of the Sexes

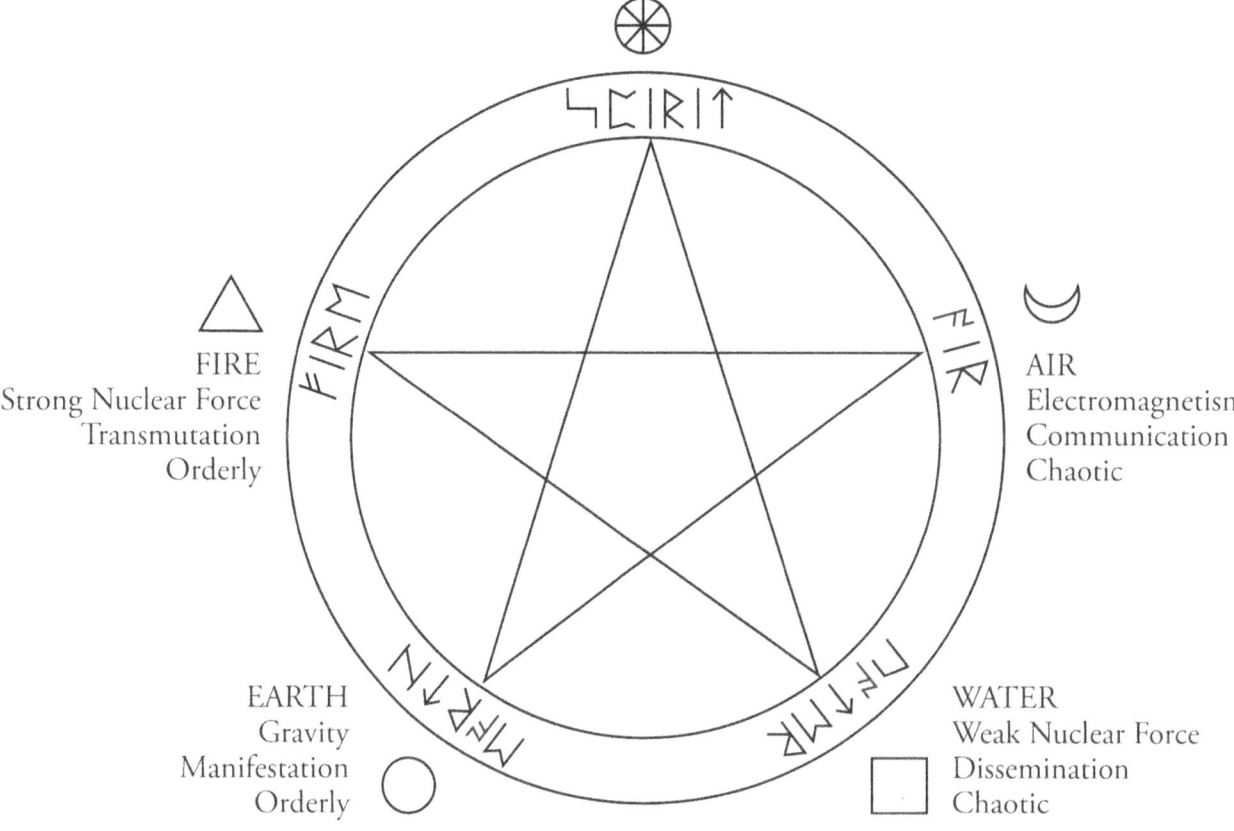
Magic Circle with Sirian Star Correspondences

FIRE
Strong Nuclear Force
Transmutation
Orderly

AIR
Electromagnetism
Communication
Chaotic

EARTH
Gravity
Manifestation
Orderly

WATER
Weak Nuclear Force
Dissemination
Chaotic

Time / Eternity

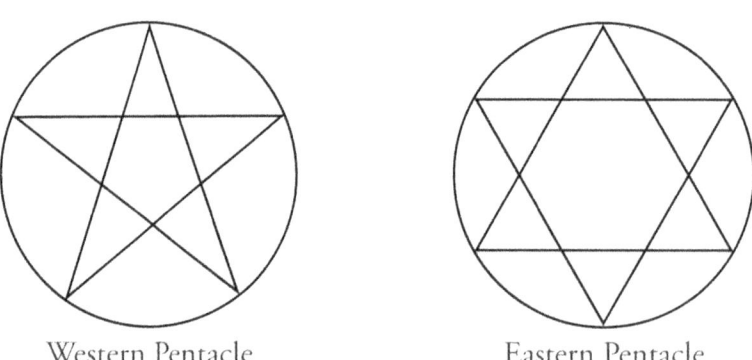

Western Pentacle

Eastern Pentacle

Pentagram and Pentacle

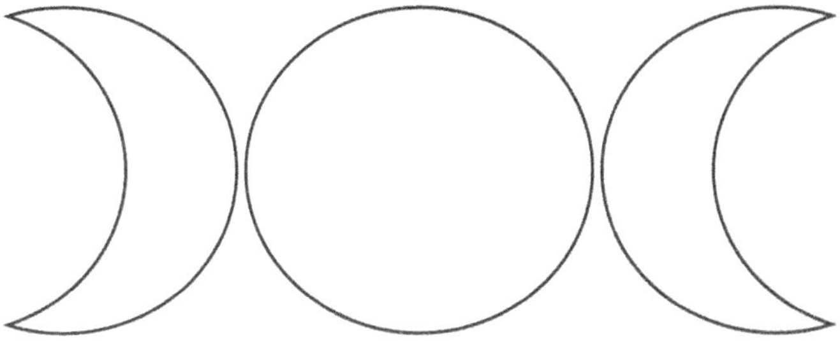

POSTMODERN WORLD

Triple Goddess

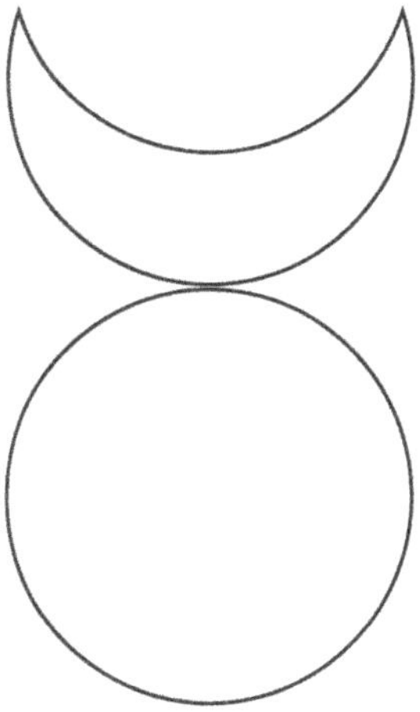

Horned God

Gardner's Pentagram - Gerald Gardner, Founder of Wicca

Dianic Wicca - Feminist Witchcraft

Wiccan and Dianic Wiccan Symbols

The Divine Feminine

POSTMODERN WORLD

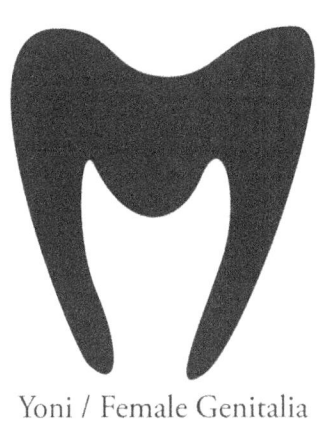

Yoni / Female Genitalia
Shakti

Asase Ye Duru
Mother Earth

Tapuat
Mother and Child

Mother Nature
(Tortuga/Turtle)

Motherhood

Mother Nature
(Gaia)

Cowrie Shell
Female Genitalia

Love Knot

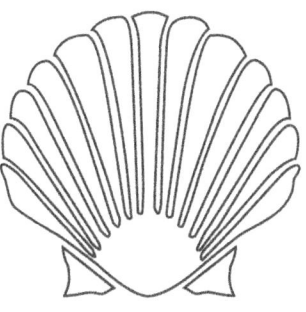

Scallop Shell
Moon / Eternal Feminine

Nature and the Feminine

Counter Culture / New Age - Western

POSTMODERN WORLD

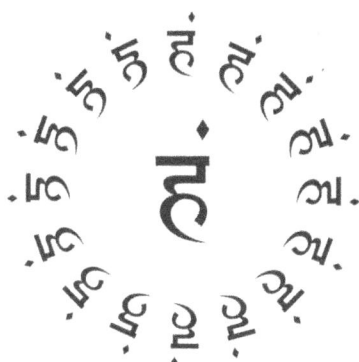

Hum - Mantra Chakra
Hinduism

Mantra Bija - AUM / Om
Hinduism

Mantra - Om Mani Padme Hum
Honourific Uchen Script
Tibetan Buddhism

Cho Ku Rei
Reiki Symbol

Mind, Body, Spirit

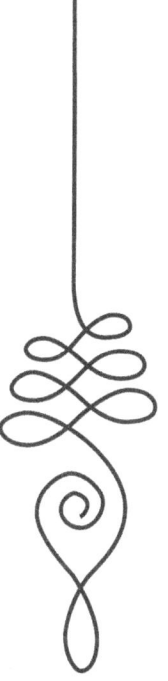

Umalome
Thai Biddhism

Double Happiness
Feng Shui

Eight Life Aspirations School
Western Feng Shuil

Shou
Feng Shui

Counter Culture / New Age - Eastern

97

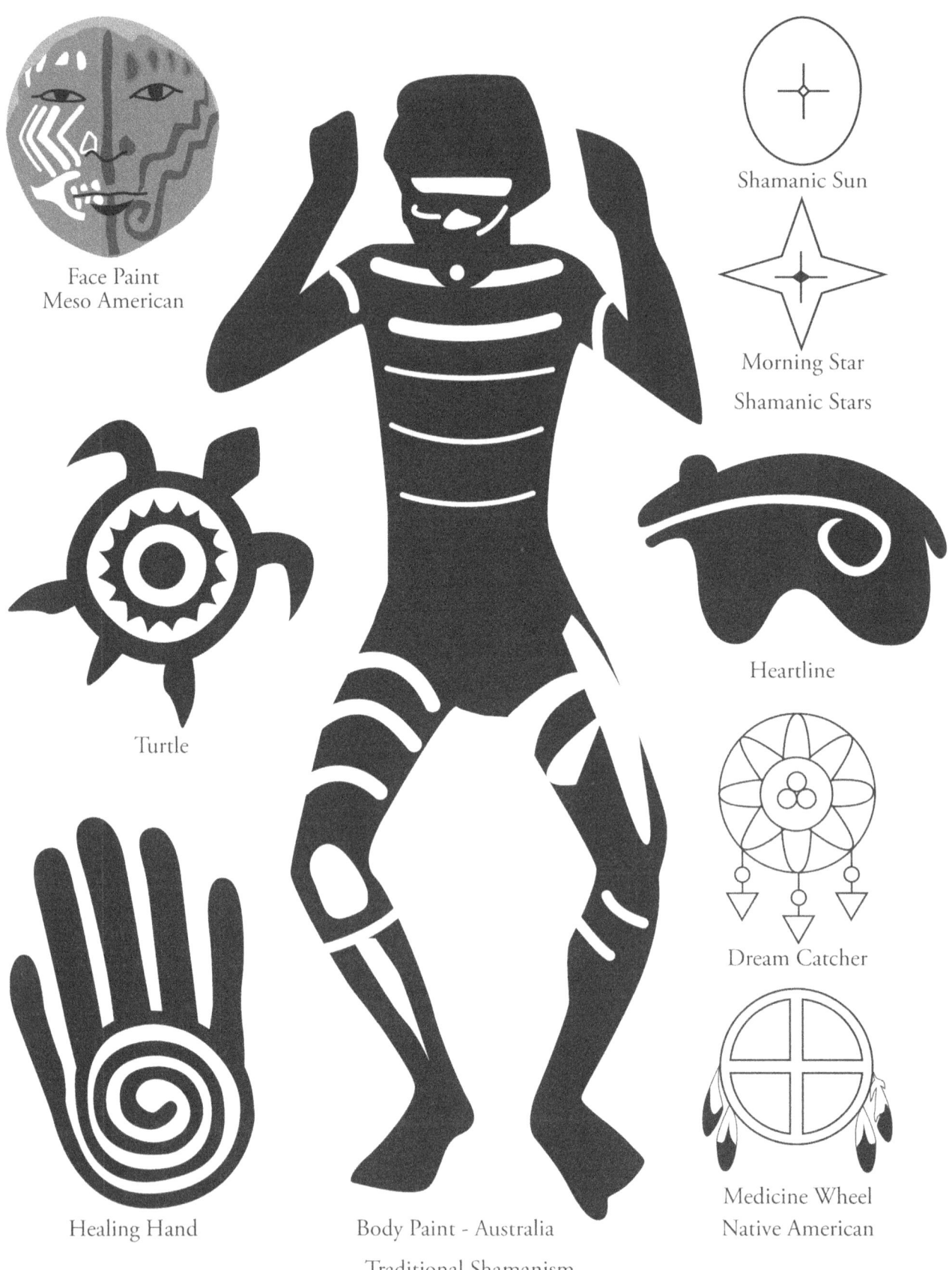

POSTMODERN WORLD

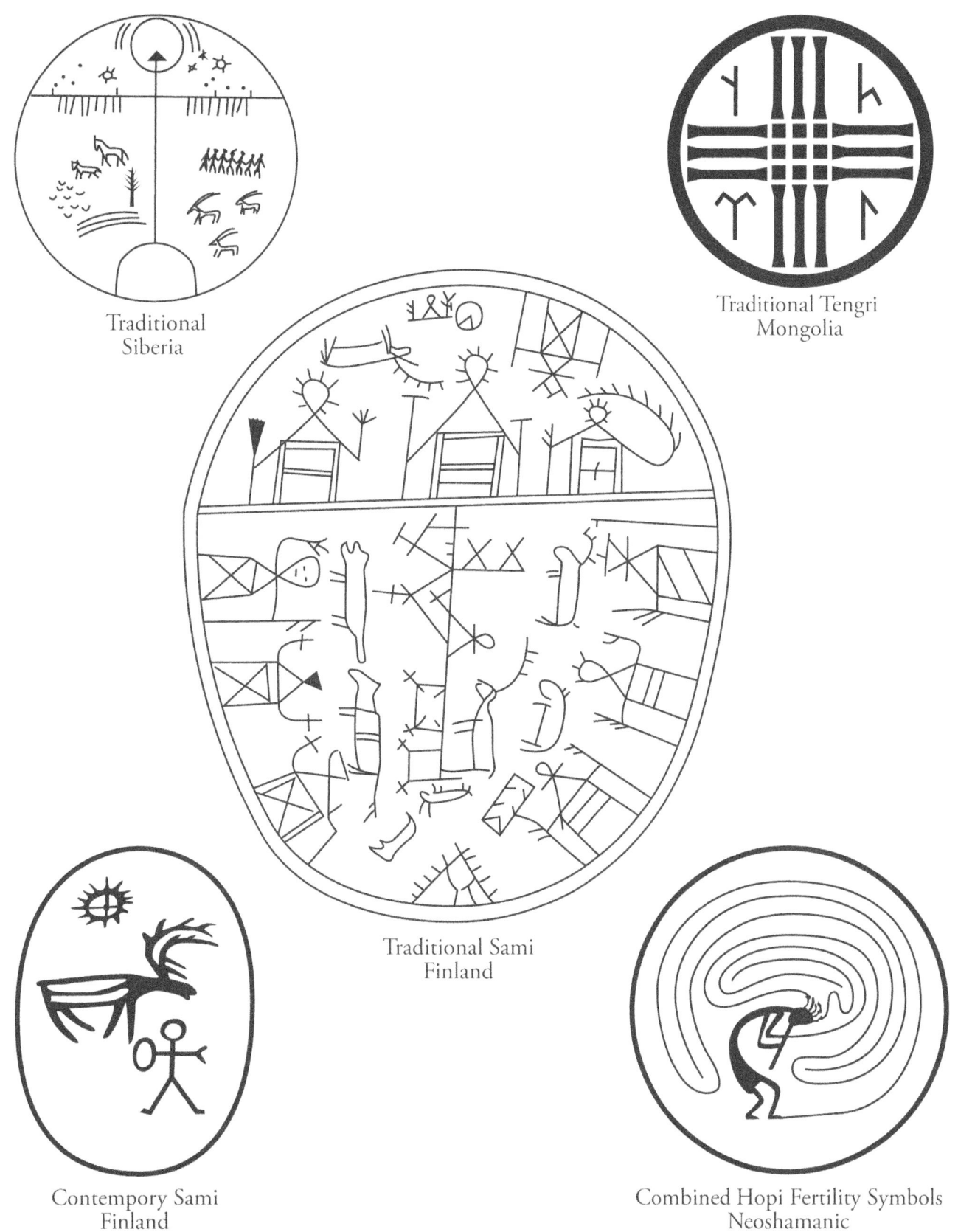

Traditional
Siberia

Traditional Tengri
Mongolia

Traditional Sami
Finland

Contempory Sami
Finland

Combined Hopi Fertility Symbols
Neoshamanic

Shamanic Drums

SIGILLAGRAPHIA

Sulphur
Brimstone

Sulpher / Brimstone
Leviathan Cross / Satan's Cross

Sulphur
Brimstone

Phosphorous

Sulphur
Brimstone

Luciferian Sigils

100

Satanic Sigils

SIGILLAGRAPHIA

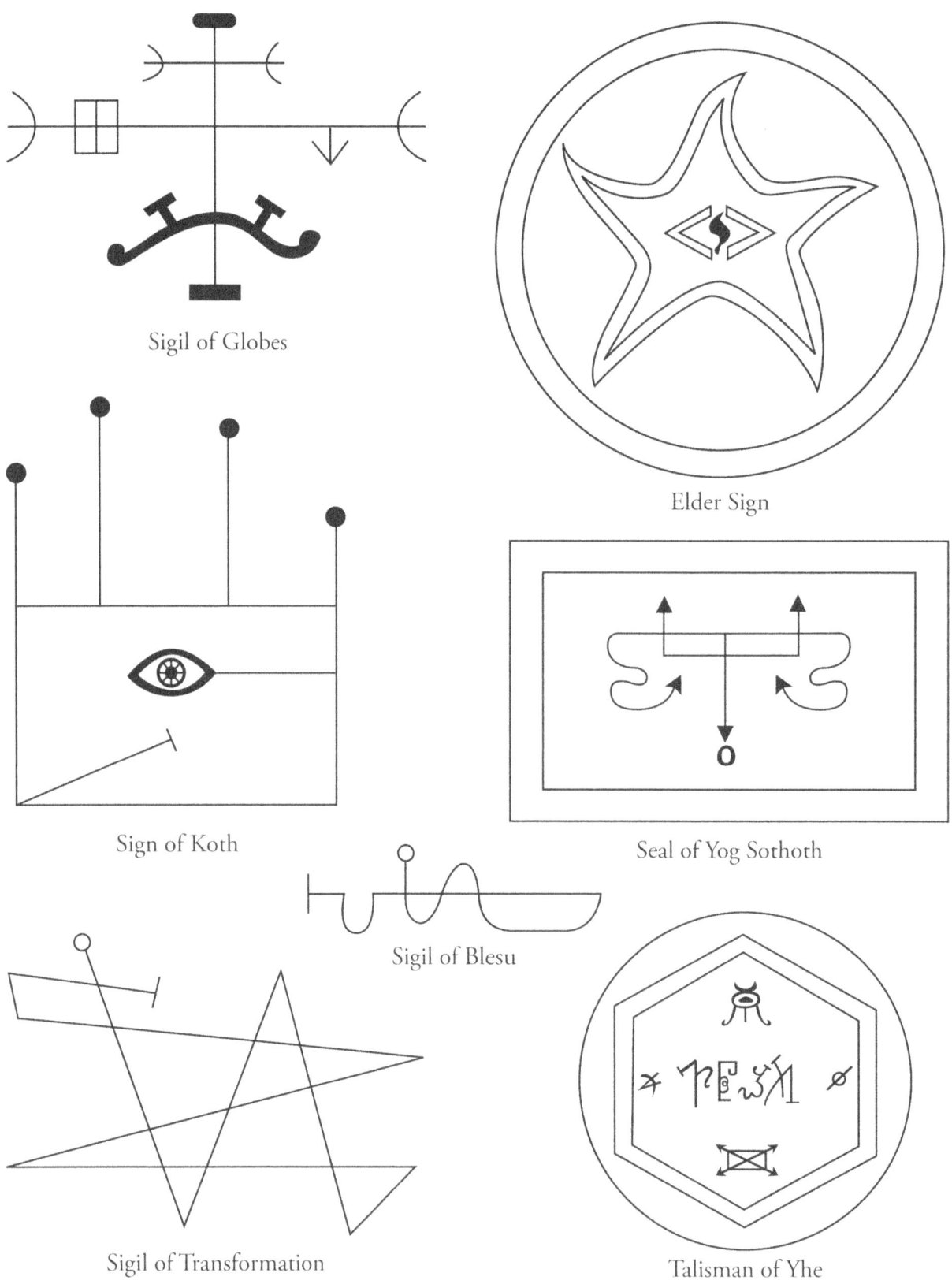

Sigil of Globes

Elder Sign

Sign of Koth

Seal of Yog Sothoth

Sigil of Blesu

Sigil of Transformation

Talisman of Yhe

'Al Azif' Necronomicon - Wilson, Hay, Turner, Langford

POSTMODERN WORLD

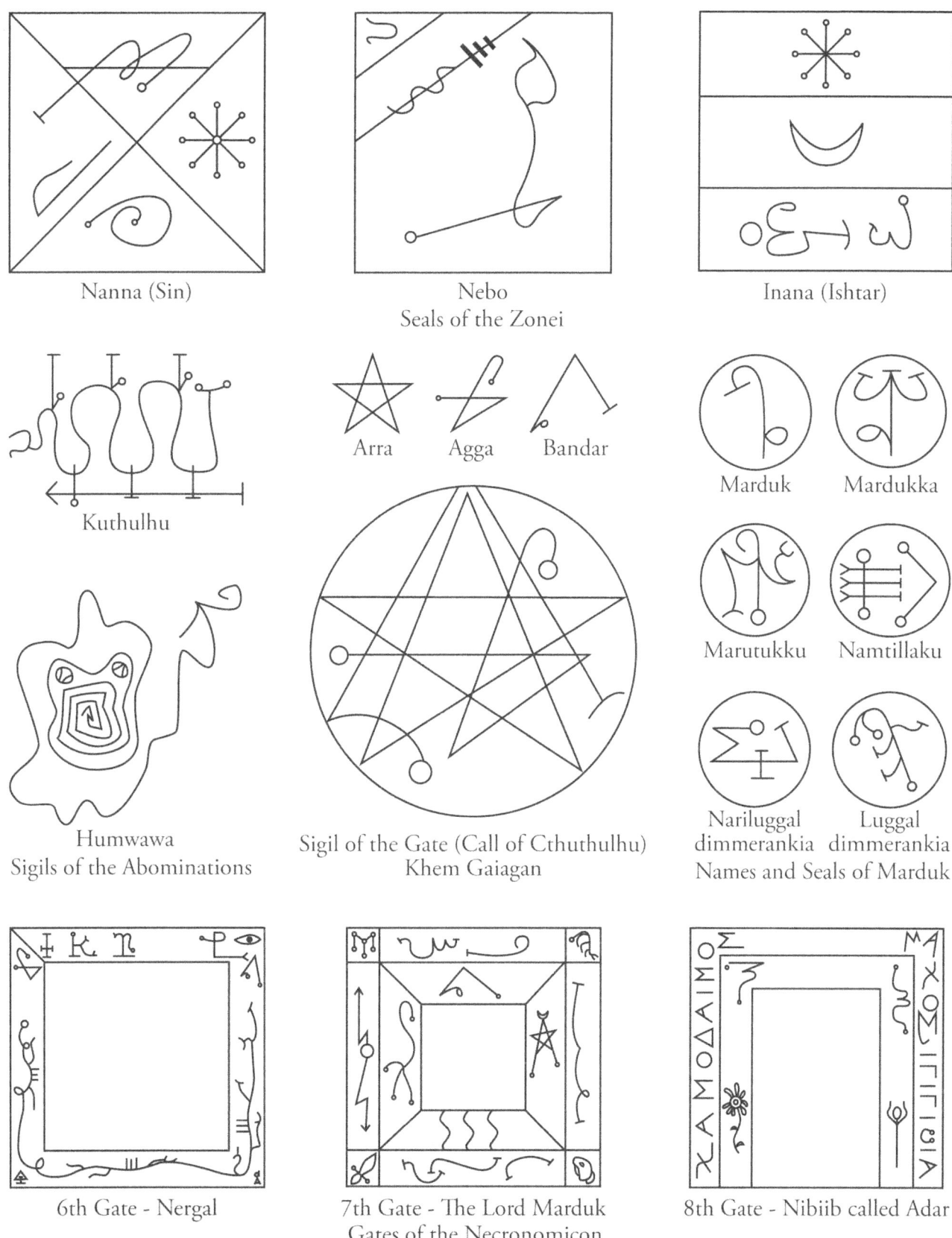

Nanna (Sin)

Nebo
Seals of the Zonei

Inana (Ishtar)

Kuthulhu

Arra   Agga   Bandar

Marduk   Mardukka

Marutukku   Namtillaku

Humwawa
Sigils of the Abominations

Sigil of the Gate (Call of Cthuthulhu)
Khem Gaiagan

Nariluggal   Luggal
dimmerankia   dimmerankia
Names and Seals of Marduk

6th Gate - Nergal

7th Gate - The Lord Marduk
Gates of the Necronomicon

8th Gate - Nibiib called Adar

'Simon' Necronomicon - Simon

103

SIGILLAGRAPHIA

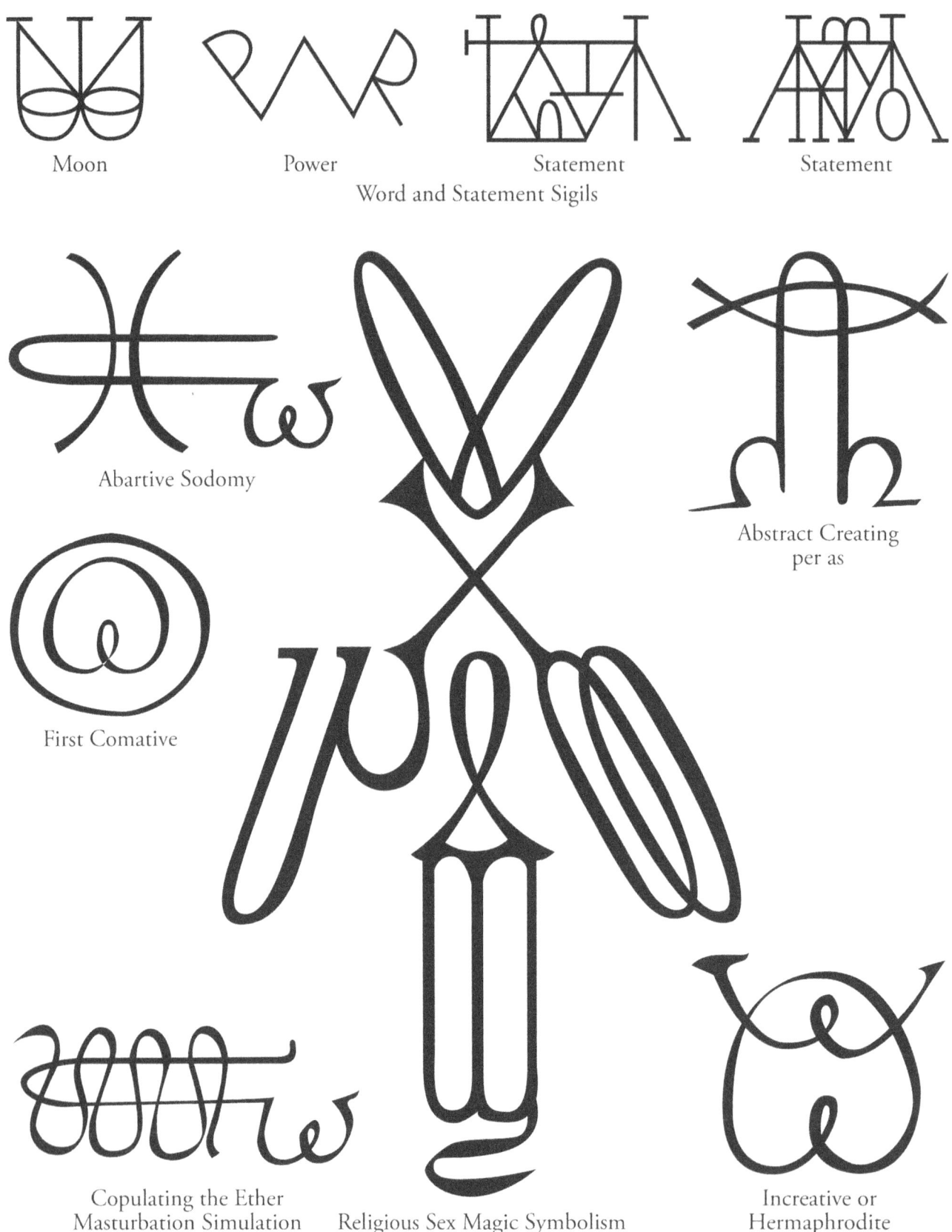

Moon • Power • Statement • Statement
Word and Statement Sigils

Abartive Sodomy

Abstract Creating per as

First Comative

Copulating the Ether Masturbation Simulation • Religious Sex Magic Symbolism • Increative or Hermaphrodite

Austin Osman Square - Sigilization and Zos Kia Cultus

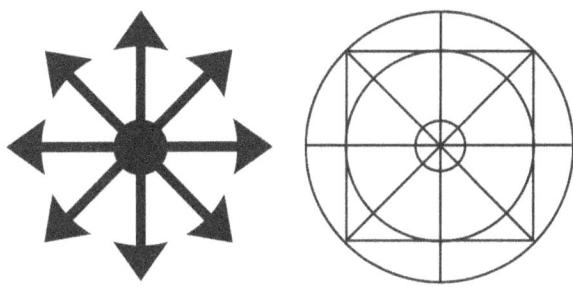
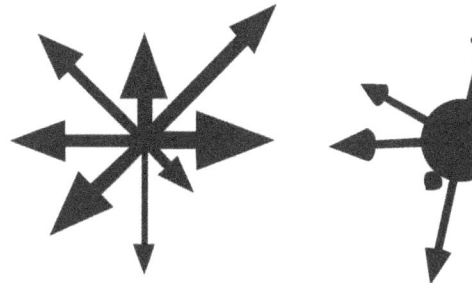

Chaos Star and Schema   Illuminates of Thanatos   Chaos Sphere / Propellor

Chaos Star Variants

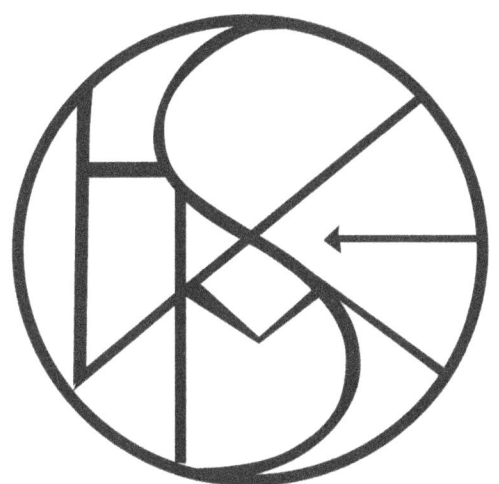
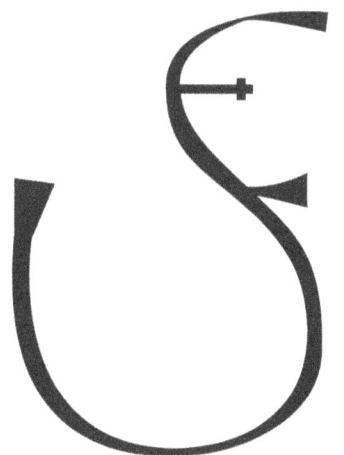

CHOSMGIK   Success   I D E S R W O L D P A C
Chaos Magick   I Desire World Peace

Word and Statement Sigils

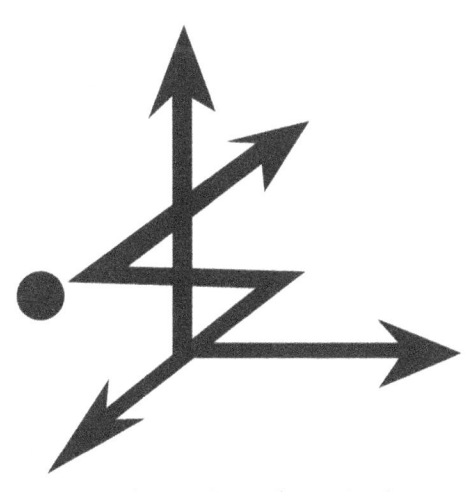

                          LS (ELLIS) Linking Sigil   633 Doombringer

Sigil Shoal   DMKU Sigils

Chaos Magick Sigils

SIGILLAGRAPHIA

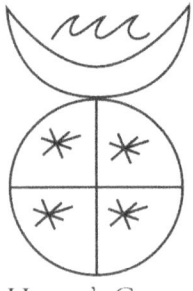
Hecate's Coven

Seal of the Harvest
MoonRaven.com

Shekinnah
Laura Tempest Zakroff

Book of Shadows
Brittany Nightshade
"May the magik of this earth flow through my veins from this day until my last"

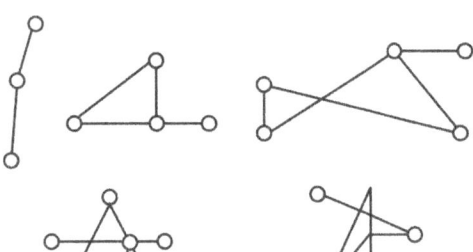
Individual Celestial Style Sigils

LGBT
Eclectic Paganism

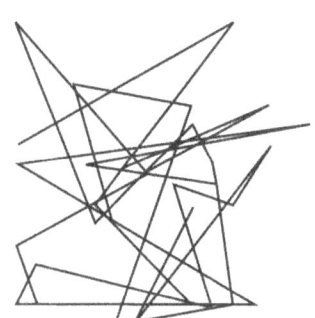
Multi Sigil

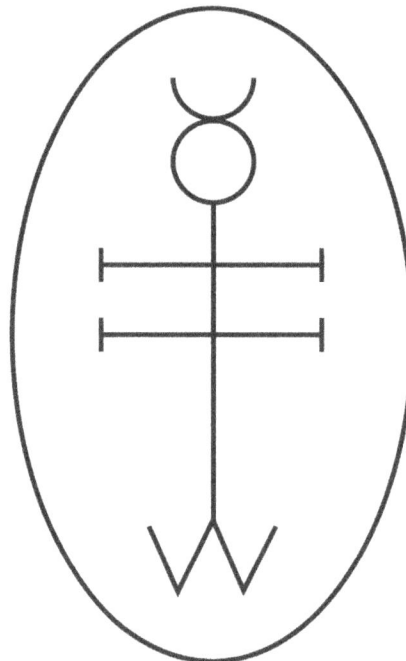
"I will get what I want"
Statenent Sigil
Grant Morrisson

Hex Putin
Michael M Hughes

Good Health

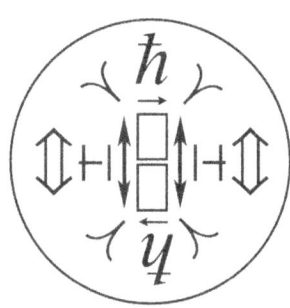
Home Protection

Rob Myers
Computer Generated Security Sigil

Computer Sigils (MT Extra)
Claire/Exemplore.com

Contempory Sigil Styles

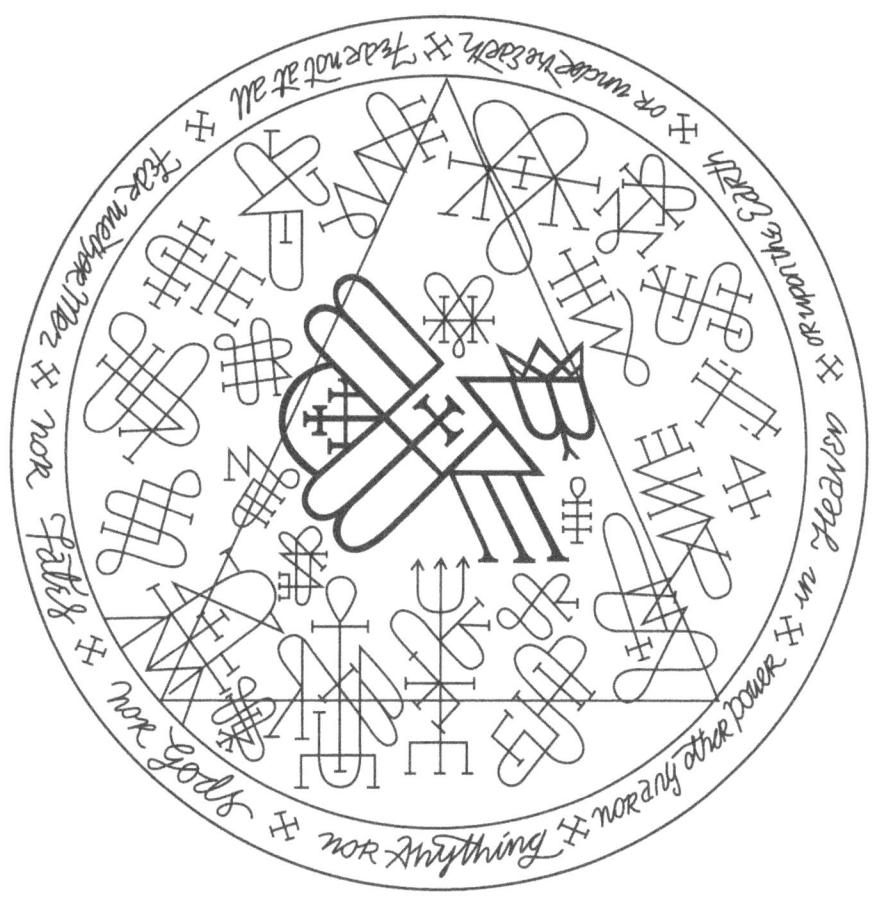

Circle of Conjuration - Sigils of Beelzebub and some of his 49 Servitors

Paper Cutouts as Sigils for Beelzebib and his Servitors

Legion 49 - William Barry Hale

New Age Eclectic Symbolism - One World Religion / World Peace

Sigil Craft

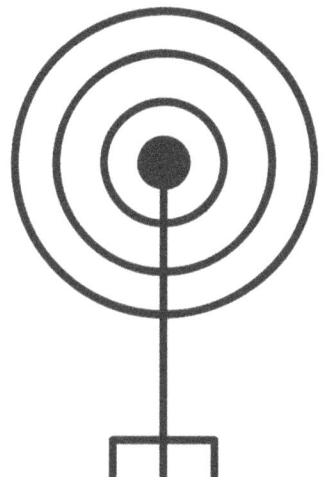

Sigil Craft

Of all the magic symbols, the most magical to draw are called 'sigils'. The term is derived from the Latin words sigilla, sigillum and signum and, in terms of magic, it is generally understood to mean sign, seal, signature or little picture. But it was from astrology that the word sigil became acknowledged as an occult device with great power.

Conventionally, a magic sigil is a line diagram symbolizing the unpronounceable name of a spirit; a pictorial signature of a spirit. To know the name of a spirit gives the magician the ability to command the spirit.

Spirit sigils are a part of the ritual of ceremonial magic used for the conjuration of angels and demons, established during the Late Medieval and Renaissance periods, 1250–1600 CE.

In the twentieth century, the sigil was re-invented as a Monogram of Thought – a graphic symbol created with the sole purpose of fulfilling the magician's desired outcome; a personal desire or set of desires. They are formed from the artistic 'binding' of the individual letters of words and statements.

For magical purposes, sigils are written or engraved onto various materials, including paper, wood, stone and metal to make charms, amulets and talismans which are burnt, kept close to the body or placed in strategic points on buildings, or in the environment for protection.

Sigils may be activated by any bodily fluid—spit, blood, urine, semen—and hidden or buried. They can be drawn in pastry and baked, carved into firewood or candles before burning, painted on rocks that are buried or set out as a decoration, or drawn in the air or in the steam on glass or mirrors.

A sigil can be made into a seal by placing it in a circle. Associated symbols and names can be added to create a polished seal.

The classic method for creating a spirit sigil is to use the numerology associated with kamea, or magic squares. This stems from the practice of Isopsephy, invented by the Greek scholar Pythagoras circa 600 BCE, in which each letter of the alphabet is assigned to the numbers 1–9, giving the letters of a word a numerical order that can be traced out on a 3×3 magic square.

The location of the numbers within the square are connected in sequence, by a line, to form an abstract figure that becomes the spirit's sigil or occult signature.

The beginning of the sigil should be denoted by an open circle, and the end denoted by a closed circle or a line. The most potent of these sigils are the ones that can be drawn in a single line without taking the pen off the paper. Spirit sigils can also be made from the artistic binding of the consonant letters of its name.

Witches and Wiccans use sigils to capture 'will' and/or 'intent', condensed into one intricate symbol. First, decide upon a key word for the goal sought in a spell. Find the letters of the word on the Witches' Wheel Cipher. Connect the letters of the word on the wheel with a continuous straight line, without taking the pen off the paper. Lines may be looped around the letters in a witches' sigil. Draw a circle at the beginning of the line and terminate the end of the line and the sigil is complete. The sigil can then be rotated and artistically embellished to increase its magical effect.

Sigils created by modern witches include pictorial devices, like moons and stars. They also contain unique signs for emotions and thoughts.

Various word ciphers are used to create spirit sigils. The Rosy Cross Cipher was created by the Golden Dawn and is based on the Double Star of the Sepher Yetzirah, providing a simpler method of constructing sigils for spirits with Hebrew names. Names in any other language will not work with this cipher.

To create a sigil on the Rosy Cross English Cipher, draw a circle around the first letter of the entity's name. Then draw a connecting line from letter to letter, in spelling order, until the last letter, when a short terminal stroke is added. The circle and terminal stroke mark the beginning and end of the sigil.

If two letters appear on the same line, a loop is added to indicate the letters. A double hump is used if a name has a double letter, or two of its letters are represented on the same petal. Once the sigil has been devised, it may be mirrored, rotated and refined. Other letter ciphers include a version of Agrippa's construction of the 5×5 kamea and the QWERTY keyboard letter order.

The occult cipher for the English alphabet is based on the cabalistic Aiq Bkr Cipher for Hebrew. It is the original box cipher for the alphabet and was one of several similar systems described by Agrippa and adapted by the Rosicrucians and the Freemasons.

As in the Hebrew, the English letters of the alphabet are arranged in a 3×3 grid. Each square of the grid contains three letters, written across and down, from left to right. The ampersand is used to equal the number of letters in the Aiq Bkr sequence.

The cipher works by taking the English spelling of the name to be ciphered and locating each letter on the grid. The letter is denoted by its position within the cell and the position of the cell within the grid. When the cipher is written, the script looks like a simple graphic design.

Agrippa described how the Aiq Bkr characters can be combined to form Olympic Sigils to encode the names of angels. Although Agrippa showed several such systems, the method shown is based on one provided by Francis Barrett in The Magus.

First, encode the name or word using the Aiq Bkr Cipher and condense its form. Next, replace the dots with vertical lines topped by triangles to further encode the sigil. To encode it further, draw a connecting line to join those letters that stand on the same line in the cipher.

Binding is the ancient technique of graphically combining key letters to form a sigil whose power is derived from the magic art of binding. Bind Runes are the most common form of this technique. Word and Statement sigils also use the binding technique in the arrangement of letters to form sigils.

The signs of the zodiac, the planets and those of the four elements can be bound together to form symbols, sometimes referred to as Elemental Sigils. Such sigils were created to represent the names of angels and, with their corresponding symbols and spirits, incorporated into the design of seals, pentacles, amulets, talismans and lamen.

A lamen is a personal seal expressing a higher or magical identity. Sigil 741 is a very specific individual application concerning spiritual families – in this case, those who consider 741 to be a dominant number in their lives. The number 741 contains three digits, so the sigil is constructed from three archetypical design elements.

The number 1 relates to the Infinite One, represented by the infinity sign, also expressing unity and oneness; the creative energy called God. The number 4 relates to the four directions or, hermetically speaking, 'As above, so below'. The X created in the centre of the two signs represents Amen. Lastly, 7 refers to the first seven of the 32 paths of wisdom on the Tree of Life. From 1, or Kether—the Final Understanding or the Great Spiritual Work of Magic—to 7, or Netzach; victory, or success of endeavour.

The practice of creating sigils made from the artistic binding of letters that form a spirit's name has been around for millennia.

In the early part of the twentieth century, English occultist Austin Osman Spare used this binding technique to create his version of word and statement sigils, which he referred to as Monograms of Thought. His sigilization technique became a cornerstone of Chaos Magick theory, developed in the 1970s, to become a staple method of sigil craft in the twenty-first century.

The common method of creating a statement sigil is to write down the intention, remove all vowels and repeat letters, then break the letters down into simple forms and arrange the letter shapes artistically.

'Goetic' is the name given to the seals of the 72 demons of King Solomon, They take their name from the book titled 'Ars Goetia', one of the books that form the text of the Lesser Keys of Solomon. How these sigils were devised isn't known, but a 'goetic' style can be achieved using a word sigil.

First, remove the vowels from the word 'sigil'. Then, bind the remaining consonants artistically. Mark the beginning with an open circle and the terminal with a closed circle. Mirror the sigil and bind planetary, astrological and other forms of symbolism to increase its magical power. Then, redraw the sigil using a calligraphy pen to give it that 'goetic' look.

SIGILLAGRAPHIA

```
1 2 3 4 5 6 7 8 9
A B C D E F G H I
J K L M N O P Q R
S T U V W X Y Z &

G A B R I E L
7 1 2 9 9 5 3
```

Letter / Number Values

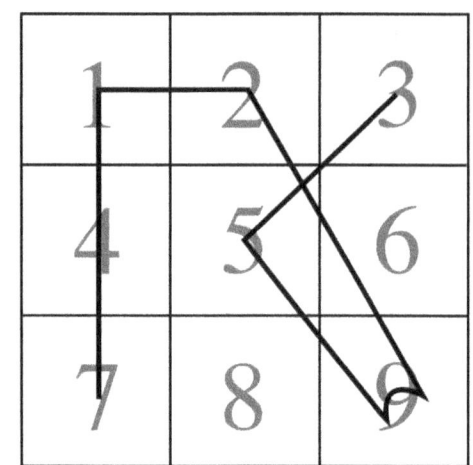

3 x 3 Magic Square

How to Create a Sigil

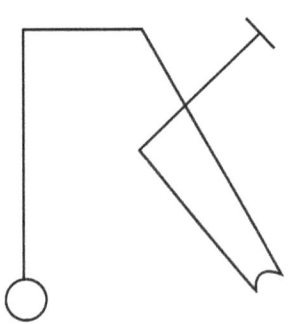

Sigil of Gabriel

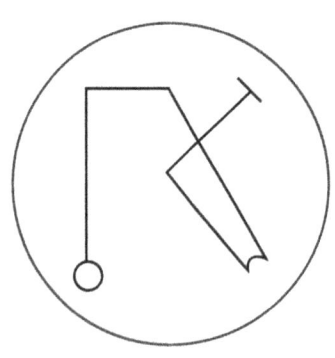

Seal of Gabriel

Pentacle of Gabriel

Sigil, Seal and Pentacle

Polished / Perfected Seal

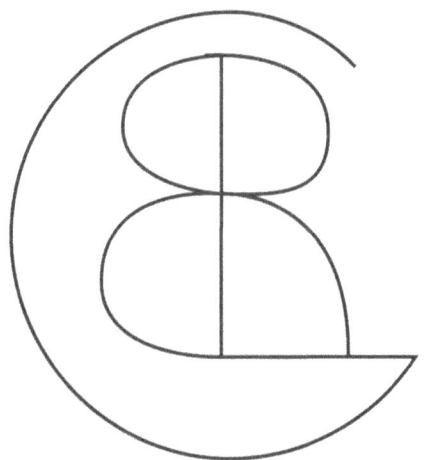

Word Sigil - GaBRieL

Word Number Cipher / Spirit Sigil and Seal - Gabriel

112

SIGIL CRAFT

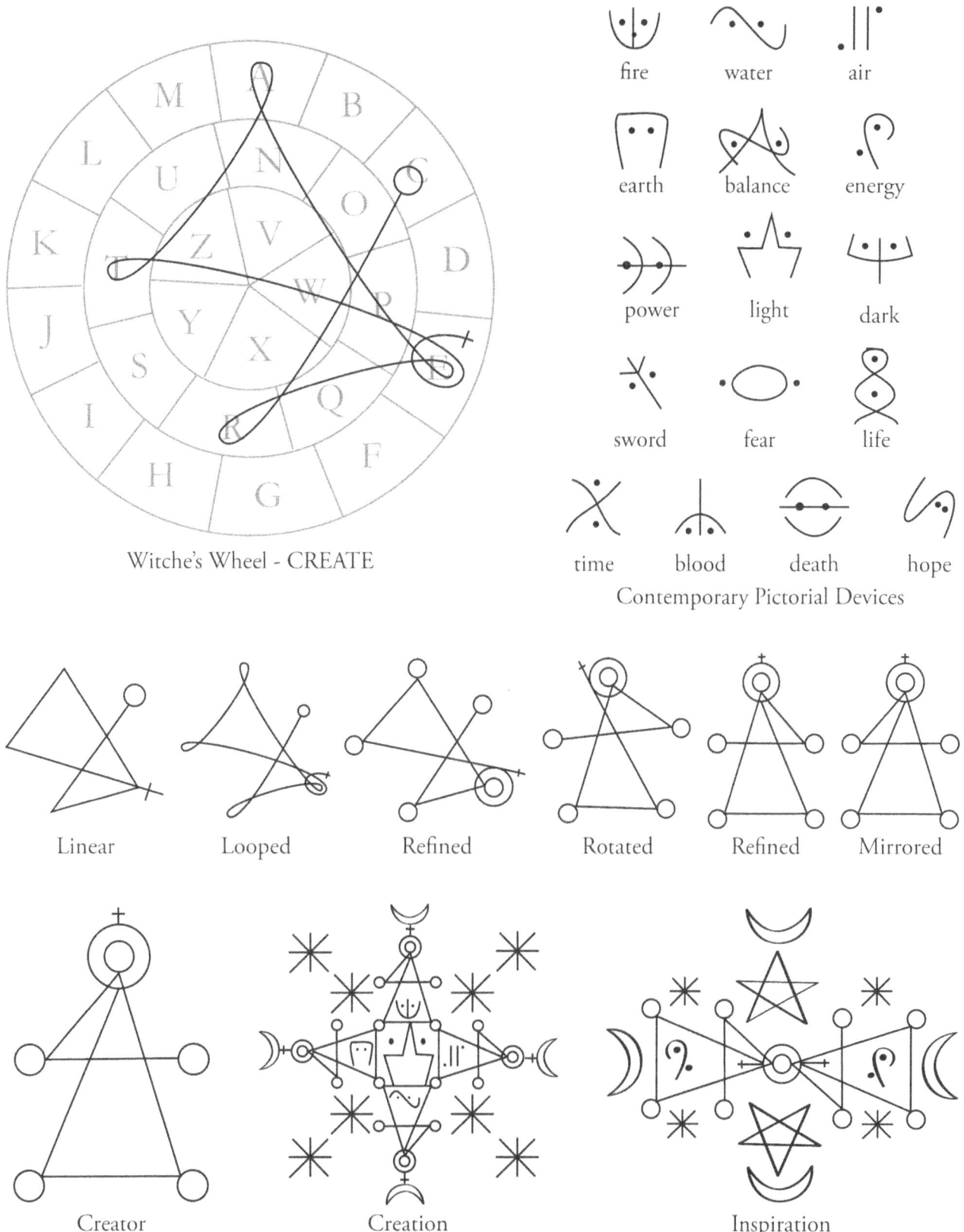

Witche's Wheel - CREATE

Contemporary Pictorial Devices: fire, water, air, earth, balance, energy, power, light, dark, sword, fear, life, time, blood, death, hope

Linear　Looped　Refined　Rotated　Refined　Mirrored

Creator　Creation　Inspiration

Witches Sigils / Word of Intent - Create

113

SIGILLAGRAPHIA

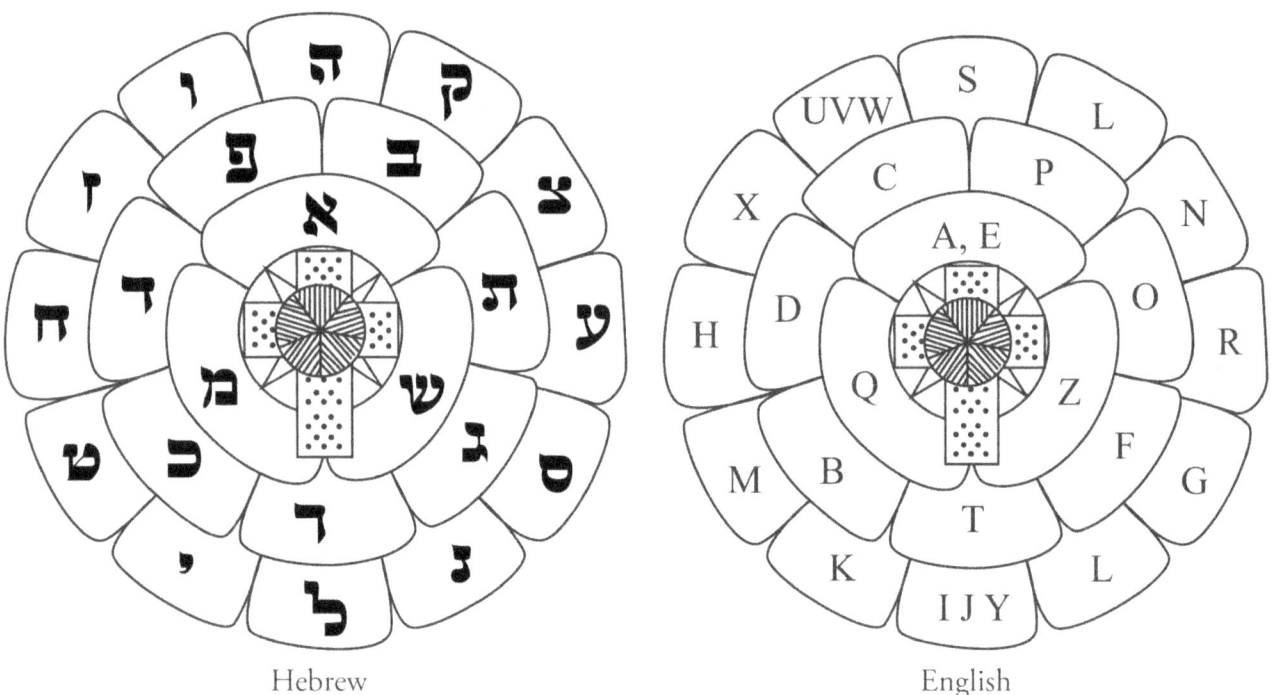

Hebrew   English

Golden Dawn Rosy Cross Cipher (Double Star of the Sefer Yetzirah)

E	R	A	O	Y
V	F	S	B	K
L	W	G	P	C
Z	M	T	H	Q
D	X	N	U	IJ

Constructed from Agrippa's 5x5 Kamea

Q	W	E	R	T
Y	U	IJ	O	P
A	S	D	F	G
H	K	L	Z	X
C	V	B	N	M

Derived from the QWERTY keyboard

Adaptation and Variation of Letter Ciphers

SIGIL CRAFT

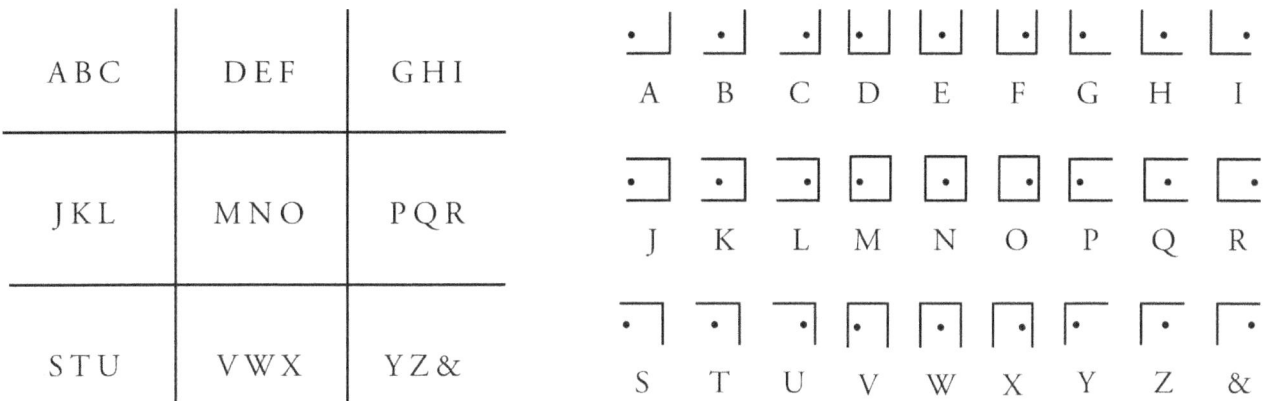

Rosicrucian Nine Chambers Cipher

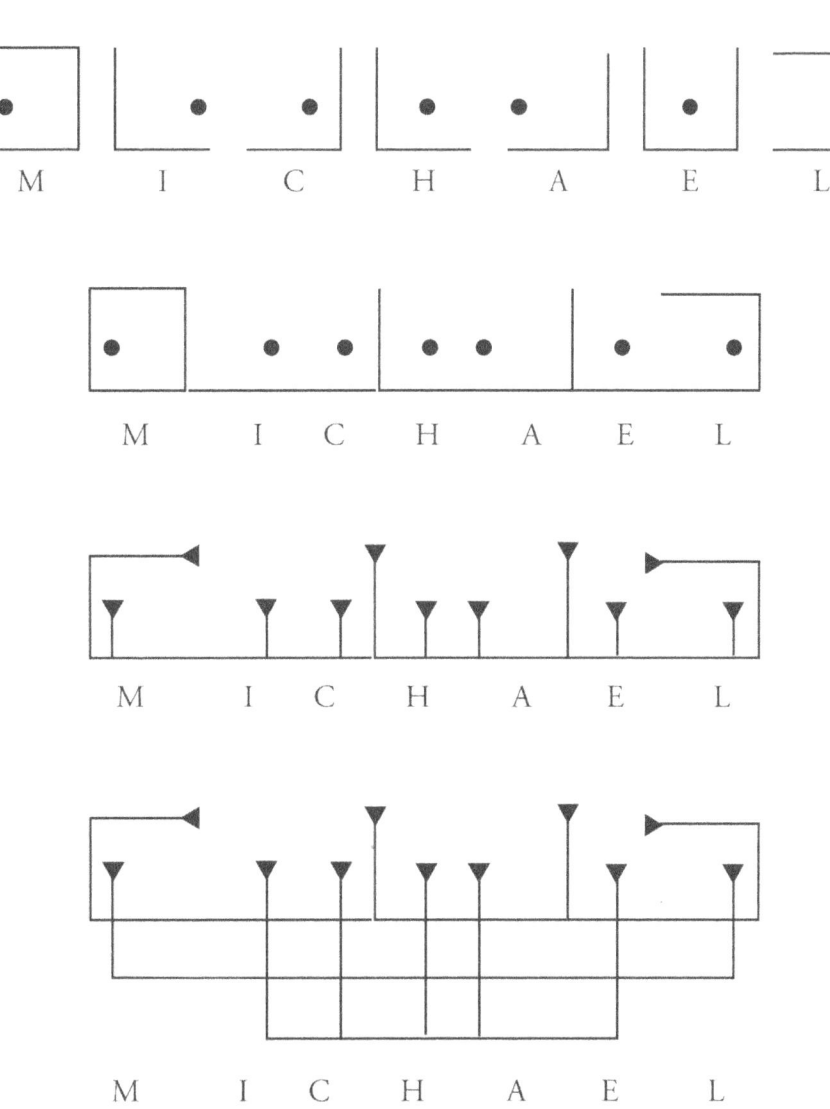

How to Create an Olympic Sigil for 'Michael'

SIGILLAGRAPHIA

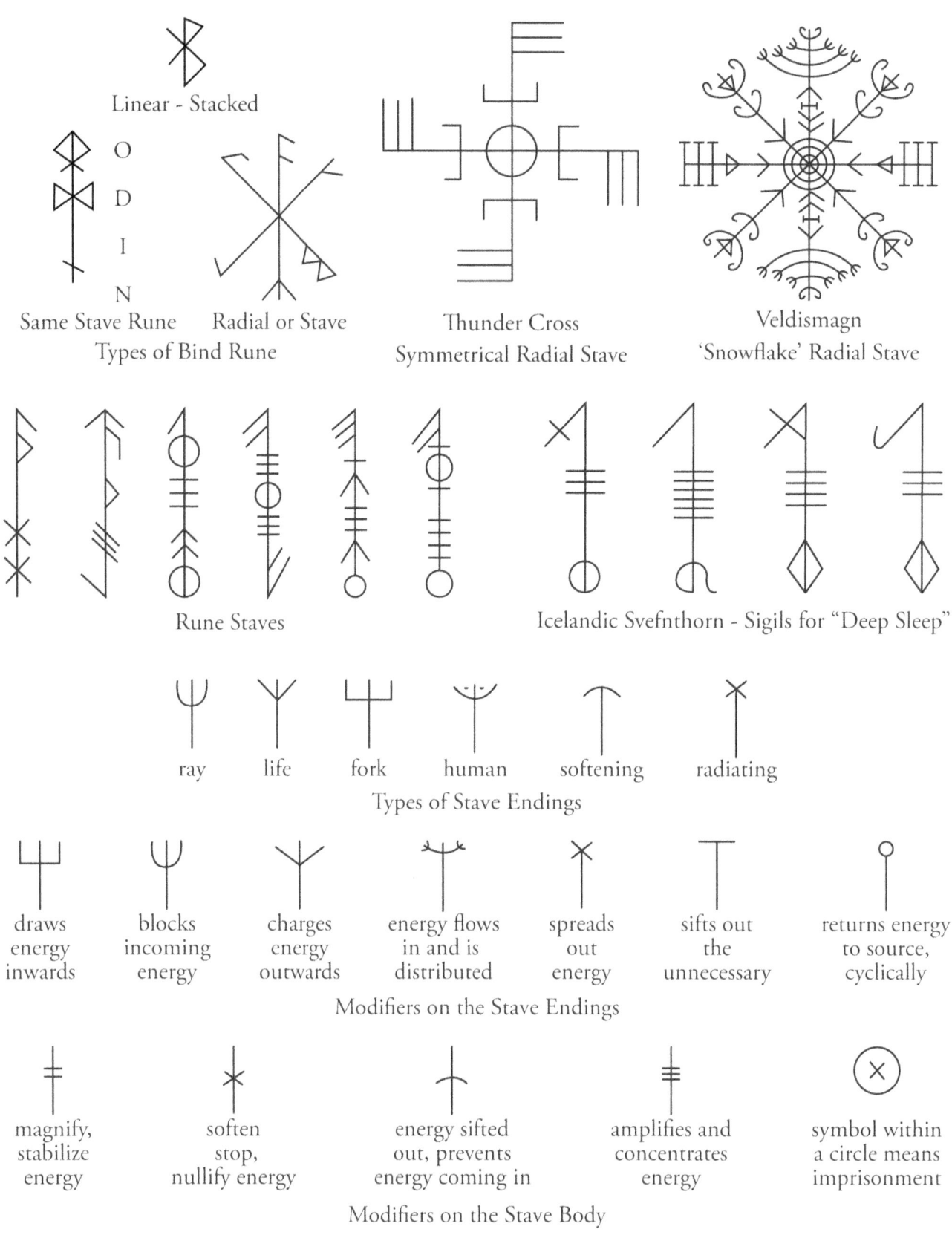

Types of Bind Rune
Linear - Stacked • Same Stave Rune • Radial or Stave • Thunder Cross Symmetrical Radial Stave • Veldismagn 'Snowflake' Radial Stave

Rune Staves
Icelandic Svefnthorn - Sigils for "Deep Sleep"

Types of Stave Endings
ray • life • fork • human • softening • radiating

Modifiers on the Stave Endings
draws energy inwards • blocks incoming energy • charges energy outwards • energy flows in and is distributed • spreads out energy • sifts out the unnecessary • returns energy to source, cyclically

Modifiers on the Stave Body
magnify, stabilize energy • soften stop, nullify energy • energy sifted out, prevents energy coming in • amplifies and concentrates energy • symbol within a circle means imprisonment

Bind Rune and Stave Modifiers

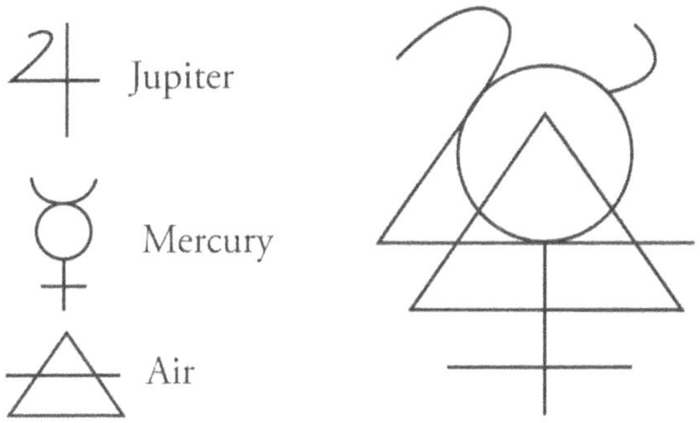

SIGIL CRAFT

Jupiter
Mercury
Air

Elemental Sigil

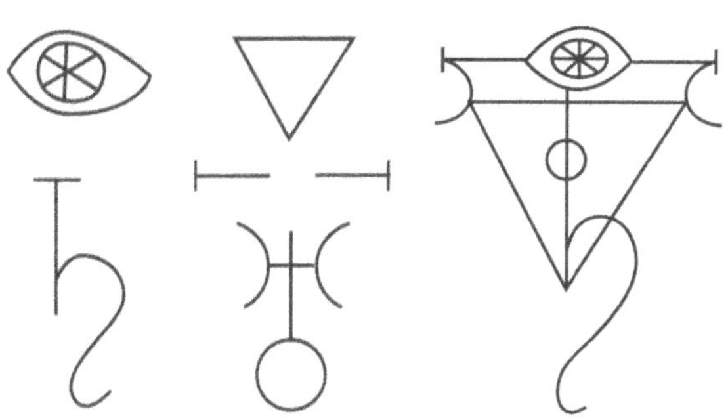

Hermetic Sigil

Seal of Aral

Center
Zodiac Fire Signs - Sagittarius, Leo, Aries

Bottom
Michael - Archangel of Fire and the South

Outer
Aral - Ruling Angel of Fire and the North

Pagan Sigil Style

Syllabae Chymica
Alchemical Syllabic Characters

Sigil 741

Binding of Symbols and Signs

SIGILLAGRAPHIA

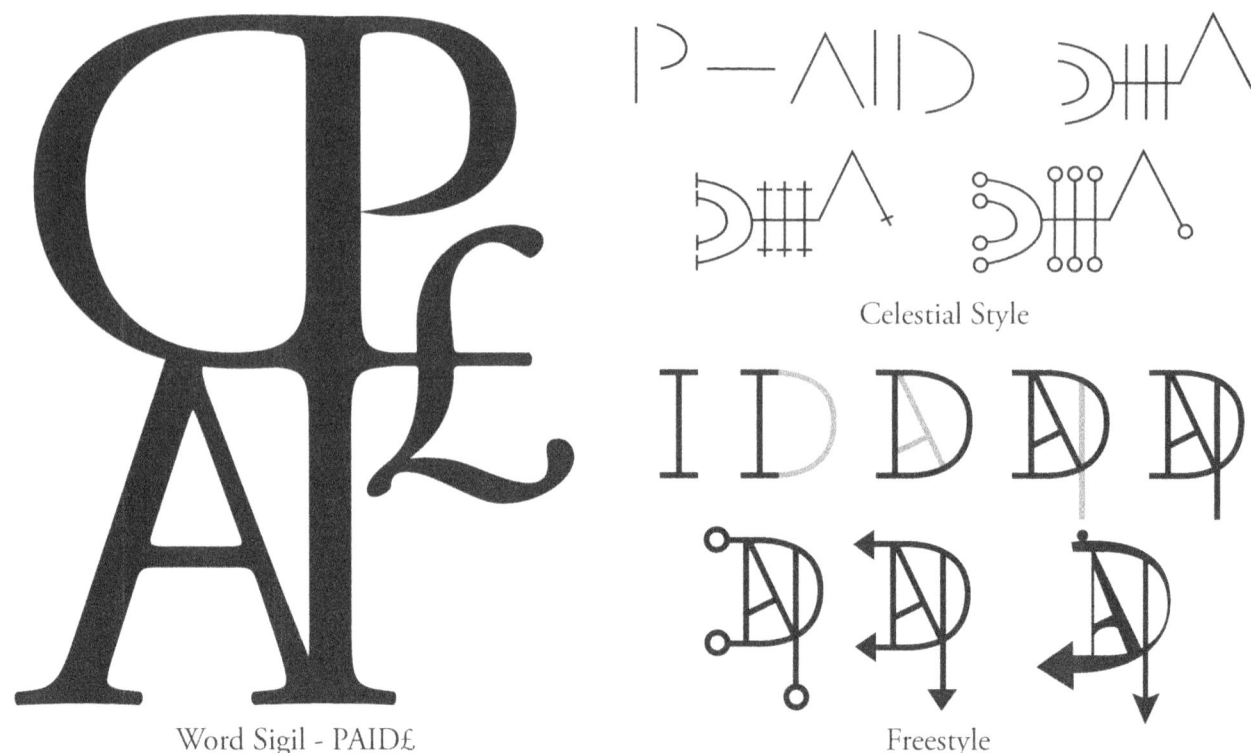

Word Sigil - PAID£

Celestial Style

Freestyle

P A I D - Word of Intent Sigil Styles

IWSHTOBANECRM
I Wish to Obtain the Necronomicon

Rearranged to Create a Pictorial Sigil

This is my Wish

To Obtain

The Strength of a Tiger

THISMYWOEALNPK
This is my wish to see a tall woman in pink shoes

Combined as One Sigil or Reduced Further

Statement of Intent - Sigil Construction

SIGIL CRAFT

White Magic | Black Magic

'Goetic' Style Word Sigil

HVNCDY
Have a Nice Day
(graffiti style vector graphic)

Chaos Magick Style Statement Sigil

Further Reading

PRINT

Hermetica
Sefer Raziel
Sefer Zohar
Sefer Yetzirah
Occult Philosophy – H C Agrippa
Keys of Solomon – King Solomon
Lesser Keys of Solomon – King Solomon
Five Books of Mysteries – Dr John Dee
Liber Loagoath – Dr John Dee
The Magus – Francis Barrett
History of Magic – Eliphas Levi
Secret Doctrine – Helena Blavatsky
Holy Book of Thelema – Aleister Crowley
The White Goddess – Robert Graves
Book of Shadows – Gerald Gardner
Witchcraft Today – Gerald Gardner
'Al Azif' Necronomicon – Wilson, Hay, Turner, Langford
'Simon' Necronomicon – Simon
Holy Book of Women's Mysteries – Zsuzsanna Budapest
Legion 49 – William Barry Hale
Liber Sigillum – Frater E. S.

WEB

esotericarchives.com
sacredtexts.com
ancient-symbols.com
occult-study.org
symbolicons.com
archive.com
wordpress.com
theosophicalsociety.org.uk
wiccaacadamy.com
gaia.com
encyclopedia.com

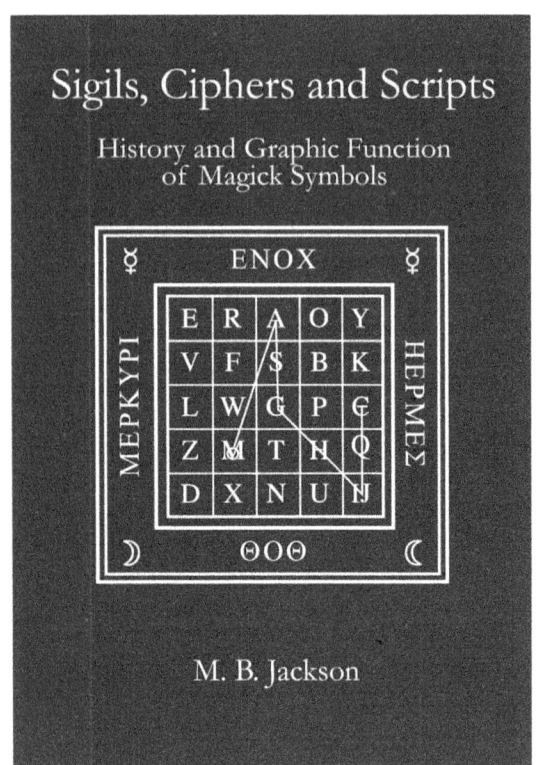

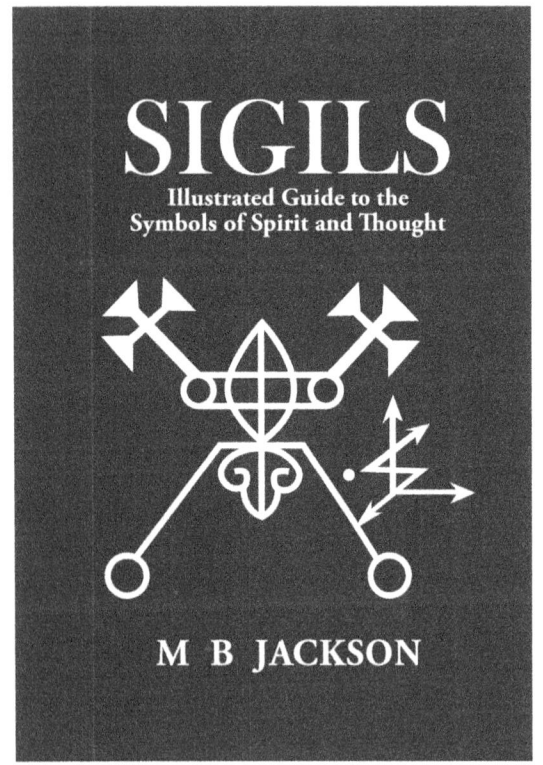
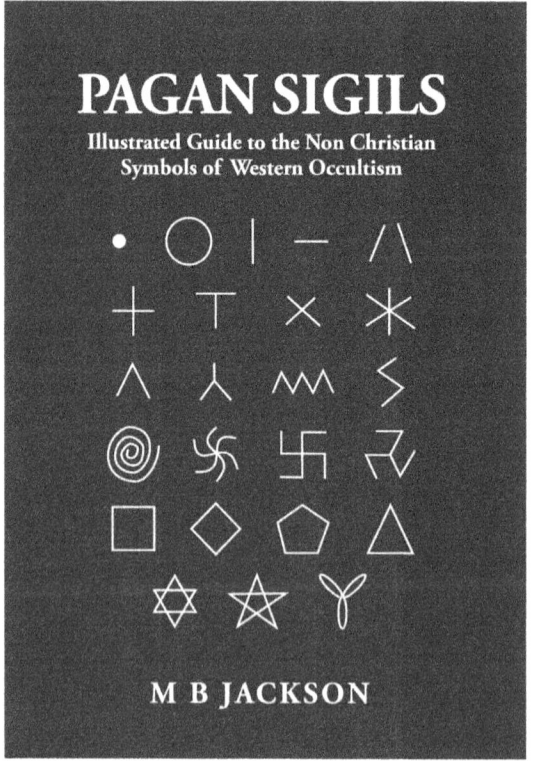

www.ingramcontent.com/pod-product-compliance
Lightning Source LLC
Chambersburg PA
CBHW080517110426
42742CB00017B/3150